Themes Pack
Copymasters

These copymasters provide graded follow-up activities for the World Watch Themes Pack. They are designed to be used to develop the children's understanding after they have seen and discussed the photographs in the Themes Pack. Many of them can be used for assessment purposes. There is one copymaster related to each photograph. There is also a further section of copymasters which relate exclusively to mapskills.

Each copymaster focuses on an important geographical idea and provides a direct link to the Geography National Curriculum, levels 1-3. A wide variety of activities are used, including naming, matching, colouring and cutting. The children can complete the copymasters working individually or in groups and can work on them in any order.

© 1993 Stephen Scoffham, Colin Bridge, Terry Jewson

ISBN 0 00 315469 6

Published by Collins Educational
London and Glasgow
An imprint of HarperCollins*Publishers*

First impression 1993

No part of this publication may be reproduced or transmitted, in any form or by any means, without the permission of the publisher.

Any educational institute that has purchased one copy of this publication may make duplicate copies of the Record Sheets and the Copymasters for use exclusively within that institution. Permission does not extend to reproduction, storage in a retrieval system, or transmittal, in any form or by any means, electronic, mechanical, photocopying, recording or otherwise, of duplicate copies for loaning, renting or selling to any other institution without the prior consent in writing of the publisher.

Design by Richard Crawford
Artwork by Julie Beer
Printed by Creative Print and Design Group Ltd,
Harmondsworth, Middlesex

Summary Grid

Theme	Copymaster	Description
Schools	1 The school building	The children label different buildings and consider the activities they can do at school.
	2 The classroom	The children link different pieces of equipment with the person who would use them.
	3 The office	The children identify the equipment used by the school secretary in the photograph.
	4 The dining hall	The children create a frieze showing how school dinners are provided.
Houses and homes	5 Houses of wood	The children join the dots to make a picture of a wooden house.
	6 Brick houses	The children identify the different materials used in the building in the photograph.
	7 House boats and tower blocks	Using word pairs the children explore their opinions about blocks of flats.
	8 Mobile homes	The children compare drawings of mobile homes from around the world.
Making things	9 Logging	The children colour six pictures telling the 'story' of paper making.
	10 A paper factory	The children complete a set of drawings showing things made of wood.
	11 Printing books	Working from drawings the children make their own 'book' of the seasons.
	12 Selling books	The children link different shops with the goods that they sell.
Moving around	13 Motorways	The children draw vehicles going on different motorway journeys.
	14 Railways	A travel game based on the journey from London to Edinburgh.
	15 Ships and docks	Using a simplified outline drawing of the photograph the children identify different vehicles.
	16 Planes and airports	The children make up their own journey using a pointer and world map.
The weather	17 Wet and showery	The children colour the places where they can see water on a drawing based on the photograph.
	18 Hot and sunny	The children throw a dice to find out what the weather is like during a period of 6 days.
	19 A windy day	Using a simplified version of the photograph the children list the 'wind clues'.
	20 Freezing cold	The children link drawings of winter scenes to the correct labels.
Caring for the environment	21 A school garden	Working from pictures the children describe different stages in making a school garden.
	22 Recycling	The children colour routes through a puzzle to discover how old things can be recycled.
	23 Looking after buildings	The children make a survey of different historic sites that their friends visit.
	24 Caring for nature	The children colour an outline drawing based on the photograph.
Our planet earth	25 The earth from space	The children colour land and sea on an outline map of the world.
	26 Europe	The children colour an outline drawing based on the photograph.
	27 Looking down on London	A dice game using six places shown in the photograph.
	28 Tower Bridge	Working from drawings the children count the vehicles on Tower Bridge.

m	National Curriculum Link	
link buildings with the activities for which they are used.	Gg4 1a)	Uses of different buildings.
introduce the idea of classroom resources.	Gg1 1b)	Talk about a familiar place.
illustrate that people need special equipment for their rk.	Gg2 1b)	Different kinds of work.
indicate how services are provided.	Gg2 1b)	Activities in the local area.
show that some houses are built of local materials.	Gg1 2a)	Use geographical vocabulary.
help chiidren recognise different building materials.	Gg2 1a)	Name familiar local features.
consider personal reactions and feelings about housing.	Gg5 1b)	Personal likes and dislikes.
show that mobile homes are found all over the world.	Gg4 3a)	Why people move homes.
illustrate different stages in an industrial process.	Gg5 2a)	Obtaining natural materials.
show that paper plays an important part in our lives.	Gg5 1a)	Naming materials.
illustrate how books are made.	Gg4 2c)	Provision of goods and services.
discriminate between different types of shop.	Gg4 2c)	Provision of goods and services.
illustrate that journeys are made for a purpose.	Gg4 1b)	Ways people travel.
compare road and rail transport.	Gg4 3c)	Different forms of transport.
help children interrogate the photograph.	Gg1 2e)	Interpret photographs.
reinforce knowledge of the world map.	Gg2 3a)	Maps A and C.
identify water in the environment.	Gg3 3b)	What happens to rainwater.
show ways of recording the weather.	Gg1 2d)	Record the weather.
help children interpret a photograph.	Gg3 2a)	Weather and seasons.
show winter weather conditions.	Gg3 2b)	Forms of water.
show how waste areas can be used.	Gg5 3b)	Improving the environment.
demonstrate the idea of recycling.	Gg5 2c)	Improving the environment.
illustrate that there is a variety of historic buildings.	Gg5 2b)	Changing the environment.
help children understand that ponds are important for ldlife.	Gg5 2c)	Improving the environment.
develop children's knowledge of the world map.	Gg2 3a)	Maps A and C.
help children recognise the shape of Europe and the tish Isles.	Gg2 2a)	Name countries of the United Kingdom.
help children recognise key features in the photograph.	Gg1 3d)	Features on aerial photographs.
illustrate that bridges are important for communication.	Gg4 3b)	Origins of a settlement.

Theme	Copymaster	Description
Towns	29 The high street	The children label drawings of different buildings and features in a high street.
	30 The bus station	The children colour and cut out drawings to create a transport mobile.
	31 Trading estate	Working from a template the children make a model of a warehouse.
	32 Sports centre	Working from pictures the children distinguish between indoor and outdoor sports.
The countryside	33 Hills and valleys	The children annotate a simplified outline drawing of the photograph.
	34 In a quarry	The children colour pictures of a quarry, mine, forest and farm and say what each produces.
	35 Working on a farm	The children create a sequence of drawings showing crops and food products.
	36 A farmer moving sheep	A modelling activity in which the animals are linked with the things they produce.
Pollution	37 Fumes in the air	Using a drawing based on the photograph the children identify four causes of air pollution.
	38 A loud noise	Working from a dozen different drawings the children select noisy activities.
	39 A rubbish dump	The children create an action picture of a rubbish dump in a rural setti
	40 Oil on the beach	An exercise comparing the way we use oil and the damage that it caus
Other lands	41 Sandy desert	The children annotate a simplified outline drawing of the photograph.
	42 Rainforests	The children colour and cut out drawings of six rainforest creatures fo a class collage.
	43 Polar lands	The children make their own drawings based on the photograph.
	44 High mountains	A light-hearted activity in which the children 'dress' a mountain mode
Children around the world	45 Getting food ready	The children colour drawings showing how rice is grown, prepared fo cooking and eaten.
	46 Watering the fields	The children link labels with pictures of water being used in different ways.
	47 A family festival	The children identify and colour pictures of different festivals from around the world.
	48 An outdoor school	Using a simplified outline drawing the children answer questions abo the photograph.
Map skills	49 Plans	The children identify where people sit on a plan of a classroom.
	50 Directions	The children show the directions of different objects from where they s in the class.
	51 Symbols	The children identify and colour weather symbols.
	52 Routes	The children trace a route past various landmarks in a maze.
	53 Grids	An exercise to create a picture on a grid.
	54 Compass points	The children colour, cut out and make a compass model.
	55 The United Kingdom	A blank outline map of the United Kingdom.
	56 The world	A blank outline map of the world.

im	National Curriculum Link	
show that the high street is the centre of a town.	Gg4 2a)	Homes and settlements.
illustrate the idea of public transport.	Gg2 3c)	Features and activities in the local area.
introduce the idea that some activities are grouped together.	Gg2 3e)	Relationship between land use and activity
indicate the need for leisure facilities.	Gg2 2b)	Describe local land use.
develop children's geographical language.	Gg1 2a)	Use geographical language.
show how some raw materials are obtained.	Gg5 3a)	Extracting natural resources.
teach children that food comes from farms.	Gg2 3f)	Location of activities in the local area.
show that farmers keep animals because they are useful.	Gg4 3d)	Large and small sites.
illustrate that air pollution is caused in a variety of ways.	Gg5 2b)	Changing the environment.
help children identify different ways in which noise is created.	Gg5 2c)	Improving the environment.
illustrate how rubbish can spoil the countryside.	Gg5 2b)	Changing the environment.
assess the advantages and disadvantages of using oil.	Gg5 3a)	Extracting natural resources.
help children discriminate key features in the photograph.	Gg3 1a)	Rock, soil and water.
emphasise that the rainforests are a vital natural habitat.	Gg2 1d)	Compare localities.
help children compare different environments.	Gg3 3a)	Contrasting weather worldwide.
highlight key features in a mountain landscape.	Gg3 3c)	Familiar landscape features.
illustrate a sequence in food production.	Gg2 2d)	Compare localities.
emphasise that water is a key natural resource.	Gg2 2c)	Contrasting locality study.
compare festivals around the world.	Gg2 3d)	Comparing localities.
help children interpret a photograph.	Gg2 3d)	Comparing localities.
introduce children to a plan of a familiar environment.	Gg1 2b)	Represent places on a map.
reinforce the notion of direction.	Gg2 1c)	State where they live.
introduce children to weather symbols.	Gg1 2d)	Record the weather.
show that a route can be identified by landmarks.	Gg1 2c)	Follow a route.
give children practice in using an alpha-numeric grid.	Gg1 3a)	Letter and number co-ordinates.
re-inforce the notion of compass directions.	Gg1 3b)	Locate position on a map.
develop children's locational knowledge.	Gg2 2a)	Name countries of the United Kingdom.
develop children's locational knowledge.	Gg2 3a)	Maps A and C.

Record Sheet 1

Children's Names

Copymaster

1. The school building
2. The classroom
3. The office
4. The dining hall
5. Houses of wood
6. Brick houses
7. House boats and tower blocks
8. Mobile homes
9. Logging
10. A paper factory
11. Printing books
12. Selling books
13. Motorways
14. Railways
15. Ships and docks
16. Planes and airports
17. Wet and showery
18. Hot and sunny
19. A windy day
20. Freezing cold
21. A school garden
22. Recycling
23. Looking after buildings
24. Caring for nature
25. The earth from space
26. Europe
27. Looking down on London
28. Tower Bridge

© 1993 Collins Educational

Record Sheet 2

Children's Names

Copymaster																	
29 The high street																	
30 The bus station																	
31 Trading estate																	
32 Sports centre																	
33 Hills and valleys																	
34 In a quarry																	
35 Working on a farm																	
36 A farmer moving sheep																	
37 Fumes in the air																	
38 A loud noise																	
39 A rubbish dump																	
40 Oil on the beach																	
41 Sandy desert																	
42 Rainforests																	
43 Polar lands																	
44 High mountains																	
45 Getting food ready																	
46 Watering the fields																	
47 A family festival																	
48 An outdoor school																	
49 Plans																	
50 Directions																	
51 Symbols																	
52 Routes																	
53 Grids																	
54 Compass points																	
55 The United Kingdom																	
56 The world																	

© 1993 Collins Educational

1 The school building

Name_____

1 Write the words where they belong.

school   house   shop   church

s _ _ _ _ _

h _ _ _ _

c _ _ _ _ _

s _ _ _

2 Circle the things you do at school.

writing   sleeping   playing   reading   shopping

2 The classroom

Name_____

1 Draw lines to show the things each person uses.

teacher

register

paintbrush

toy robot

pen

globe

child

paper

Schools

© 1993 Collins Educational

3 The office

Name_____

1 Using a ruler, draw arrows from the words to the things in the picture.

computer   boxes   filing cabinet

pens   telephone   register

2 Colour the picture.

Schools

4 The dining hall

Name_____

1 Colour the pictures.	2 Cut them out.
3 Put them in order.	4 Glue them down.

Food arrives at school.

The food is cooked.

Children eat dinner.

Rubbish is taken away.

5 Houses of wood

Name_____

1 Join the dots.   **2** Colour the picture.

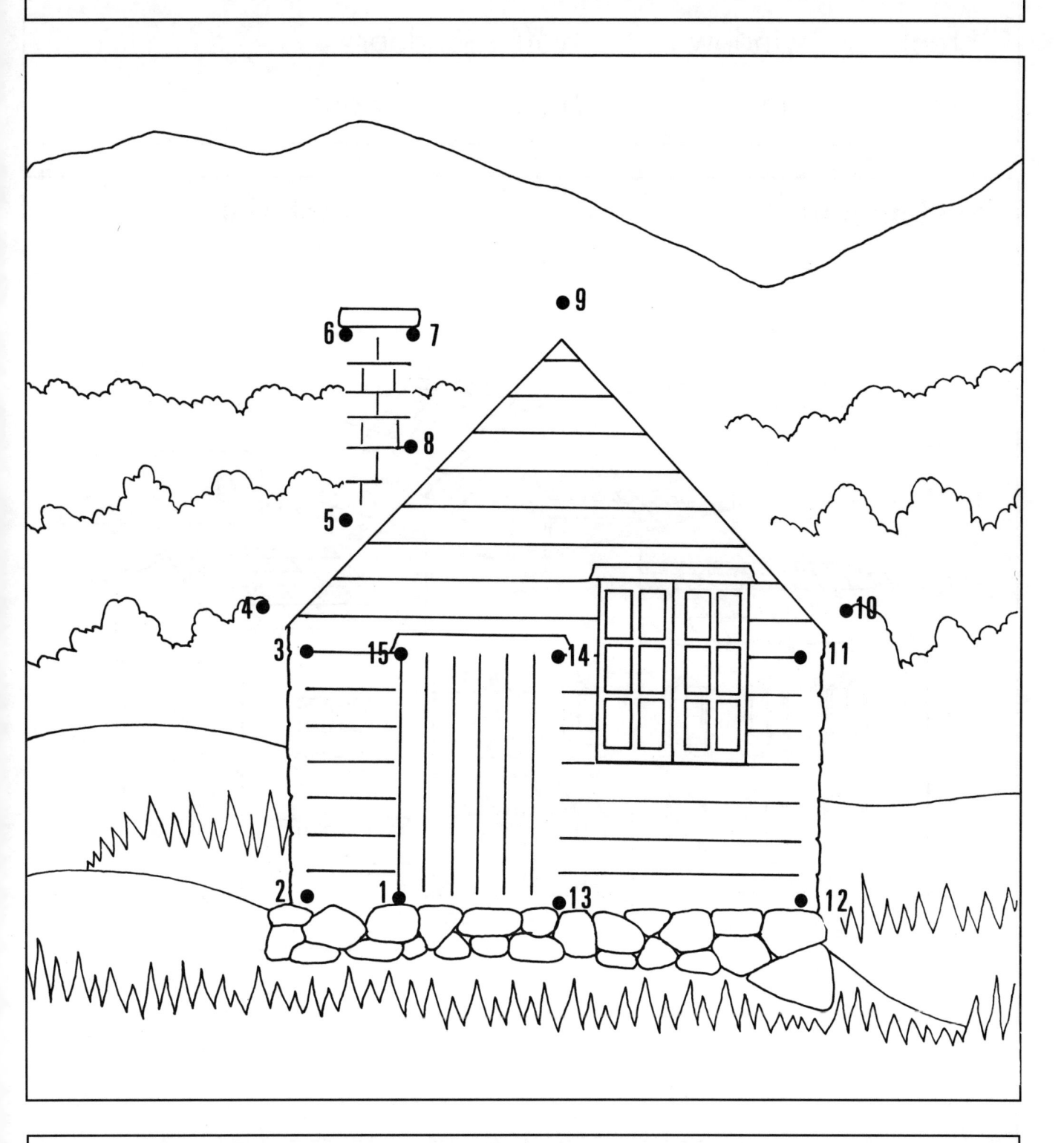

3 Write these words in the empty spaces.

trees   houses   snow

There are lots of t _ _ _ _ in this place. They help to make the h _ _ _ _ _. The steep roof keeps off s _ _ _ in winter.

Houses and homes

6 Brick houses

Name_____

1 Write the words where they belong.

roof   window   wall   door
tiles   glass   brick   wood

Building part   **Material**

r _ _ _   t _ _ _ _

w _ _ _ _ _   g _ _ _ _

w _ _ _

b _ _ _ _

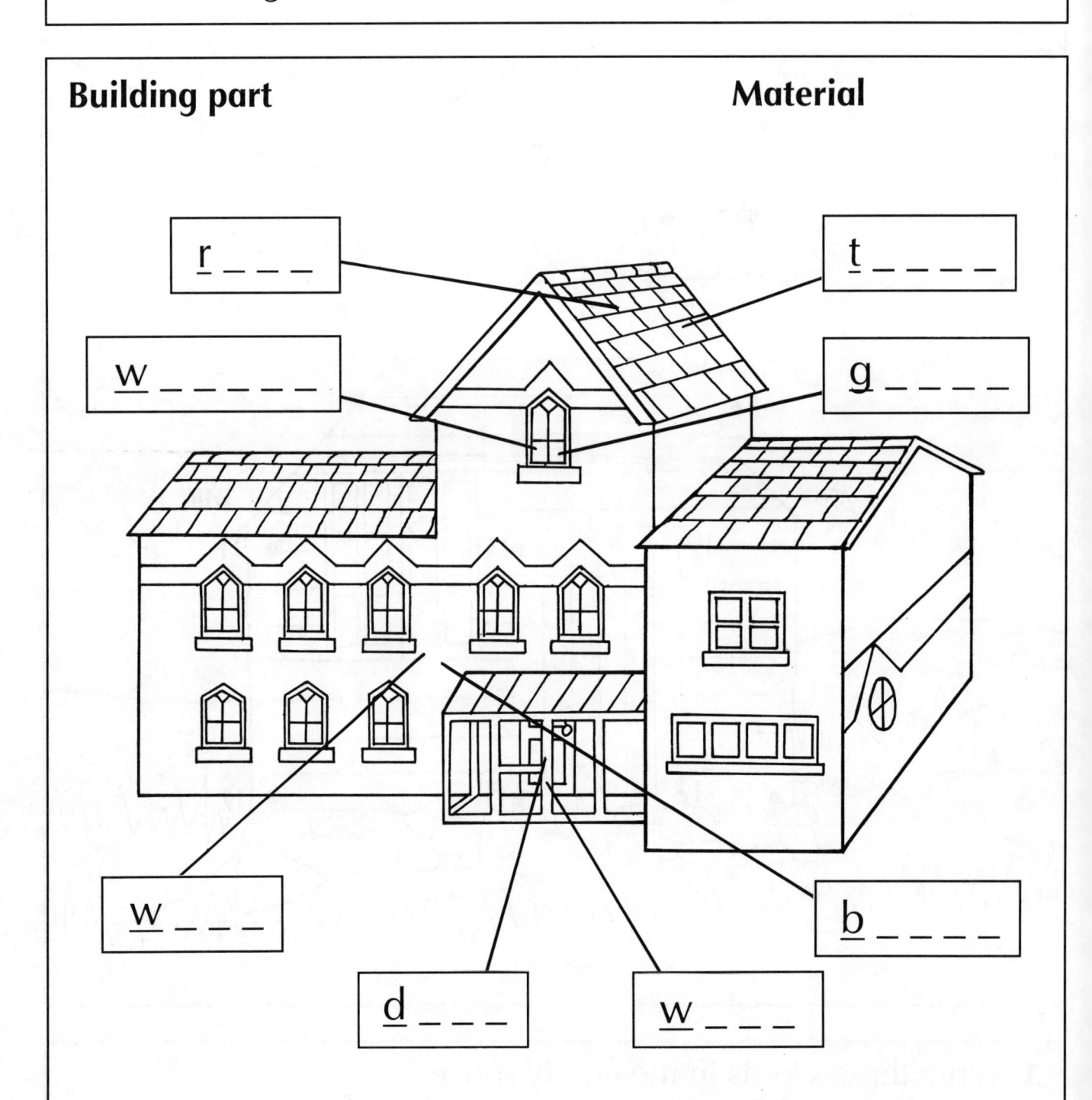

d _ _ _   w _ _ _

Lots of bricks are used to make the h _ _ _ _ _ .

Bricks are good for walls because they are s _ _ _ _ _ _ .

Houses and homes   © 1993 Collins Educational

7 Tower blocks

Name_____

1 Circle the best words in each pair.

2 Add curtains and other things to make each flat into a home.

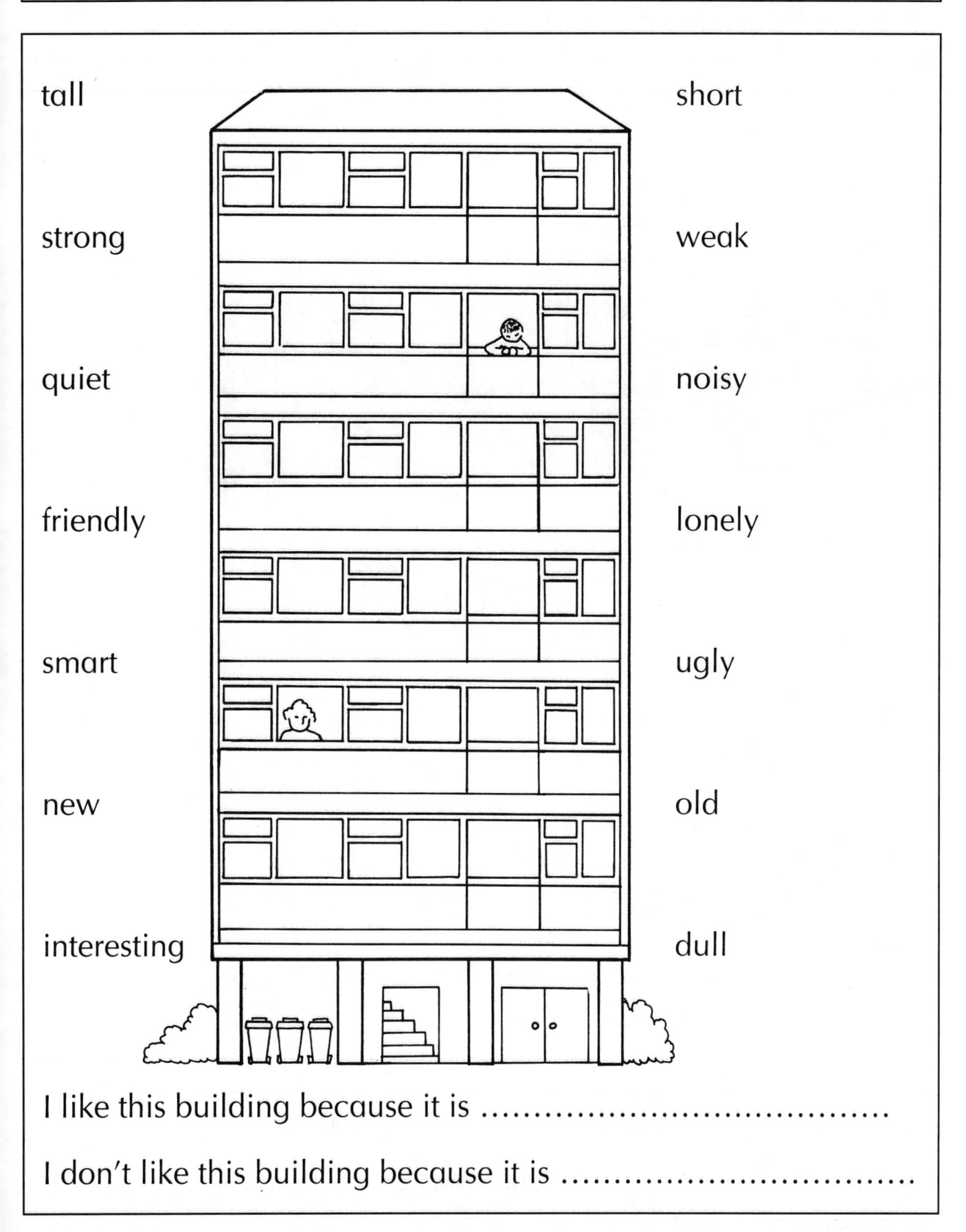

tall	short
strong	weak
quiet	noisy
friendly	lonely
smart	ugly
new	old
interesting	dull

I like this building because it is ....

I don't like this building because it is ....

Houses and homes

© 1993 Collins Educational

8 Mobile homes

Name_____

1 Write the words where they belong.

house boat   tent   caravan   hut

2 Colour the pictures.

_ _ _ _ _ _ _   _ _ _ _

_ _ _ _ _ _ _ _   _ _ _

3 Circle the homes from the United Kingdom.

4 Tick the homes from distant lands.

Houses and homes   © 1993 Collins Educational

9 Logging

Name_____

1 Colour the pictures.
2 Cut them out.
3 Put them in a row to make a story.
4 Glue them down.

PULP

Making things

© 1993 Collins Educational

10 A paper factory

Name_____

1. Make drawings of two more things made of paper.
2. Colour the pictures.
3. Circle the best words about paper.

light   heavy   smooth   rough   soft   hard

paper bag

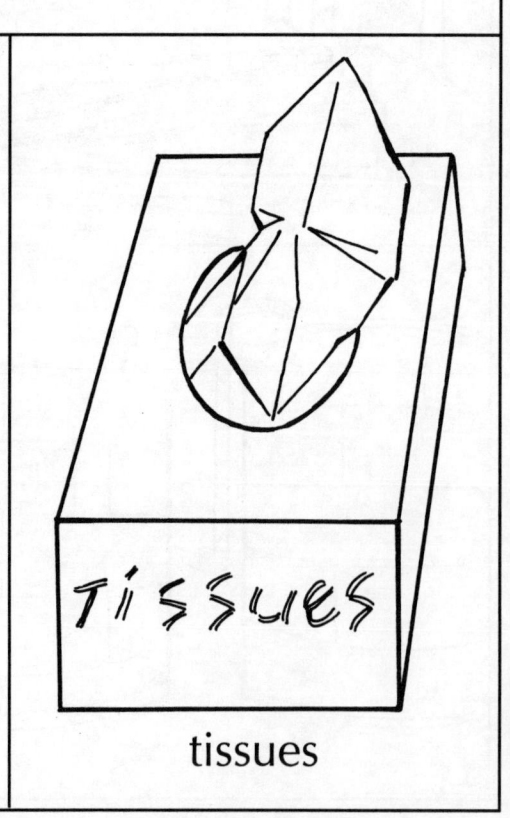

tissues

Making things

© 1993 Collins Educational

11 Printing books

Name_____

1 Colour the pictures.
2 Write the name of the season underneath.
   spring   summer   autumn   winter
3 Cut up the pages and make a cover.
4 Staple your book together in the right order.

There are lots of flowers.

s _ _ _ _ _ _

People go swimming.

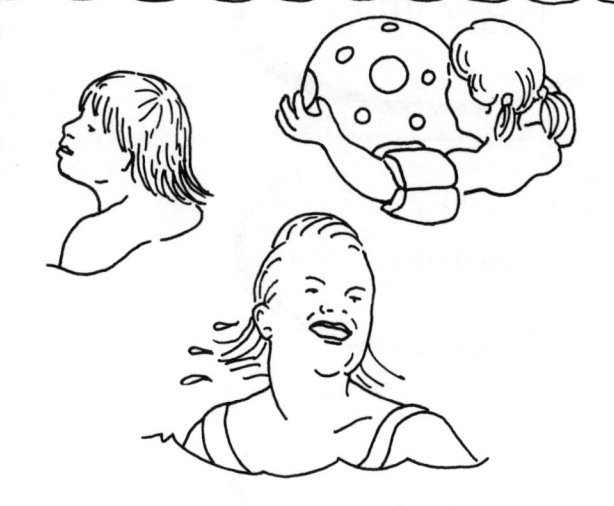

s _ _ _ _ _ _

The leaves fall from the trees.

a _ _ _ _ _ _

It is snowing.

w _ _ _ _ _ _

Making things   © 1993 Collins Educational

12 Selling books

Name_____

1 Draw a line from each shop to the things that it sells.

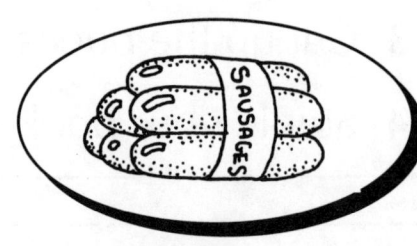

Shop	sells	**Goods**
The bookshop		(sausages)
The Post Office		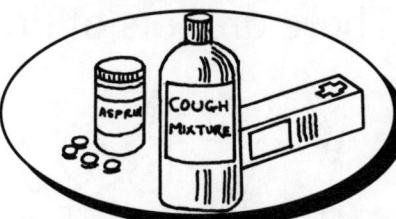 (aspirin, cough mixture)
The butcher		 (books)
The greengrocer		 (stamps)
The chemist		(oranges)
The supermarket		 (can of Coca-Cola, newspapers)
The newsagent		 (honey, biscuits)

Making things

© 1993 Collins Educational

13 Motorways

Name_____

1 Make these drawings on the picture

   a A lorry going north.   **c** A coach going south.

   b A car going east.   **d** A police car going west.

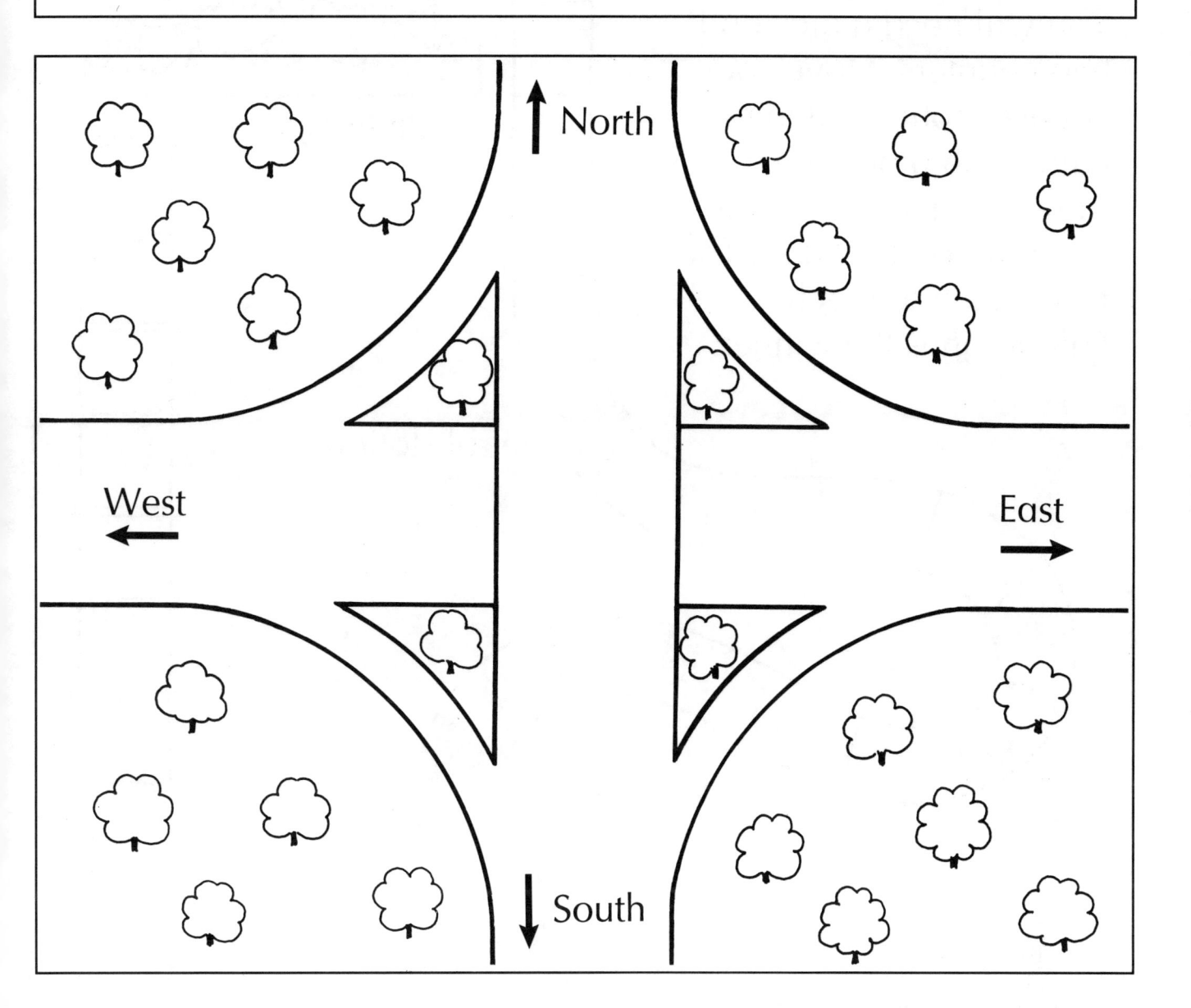

2 Write the words in the right sentences.

   factory   holiday   accident

   (**a**) The lorry is going to the ………………………………………………

   (**b**) The police car is going to an ………………………………………

   (**c**) The car is taking people on ………………………………………

Moving around   © 1993 Collins Educational

14 Railways

Name_____

1 Play the railway game with a partner.

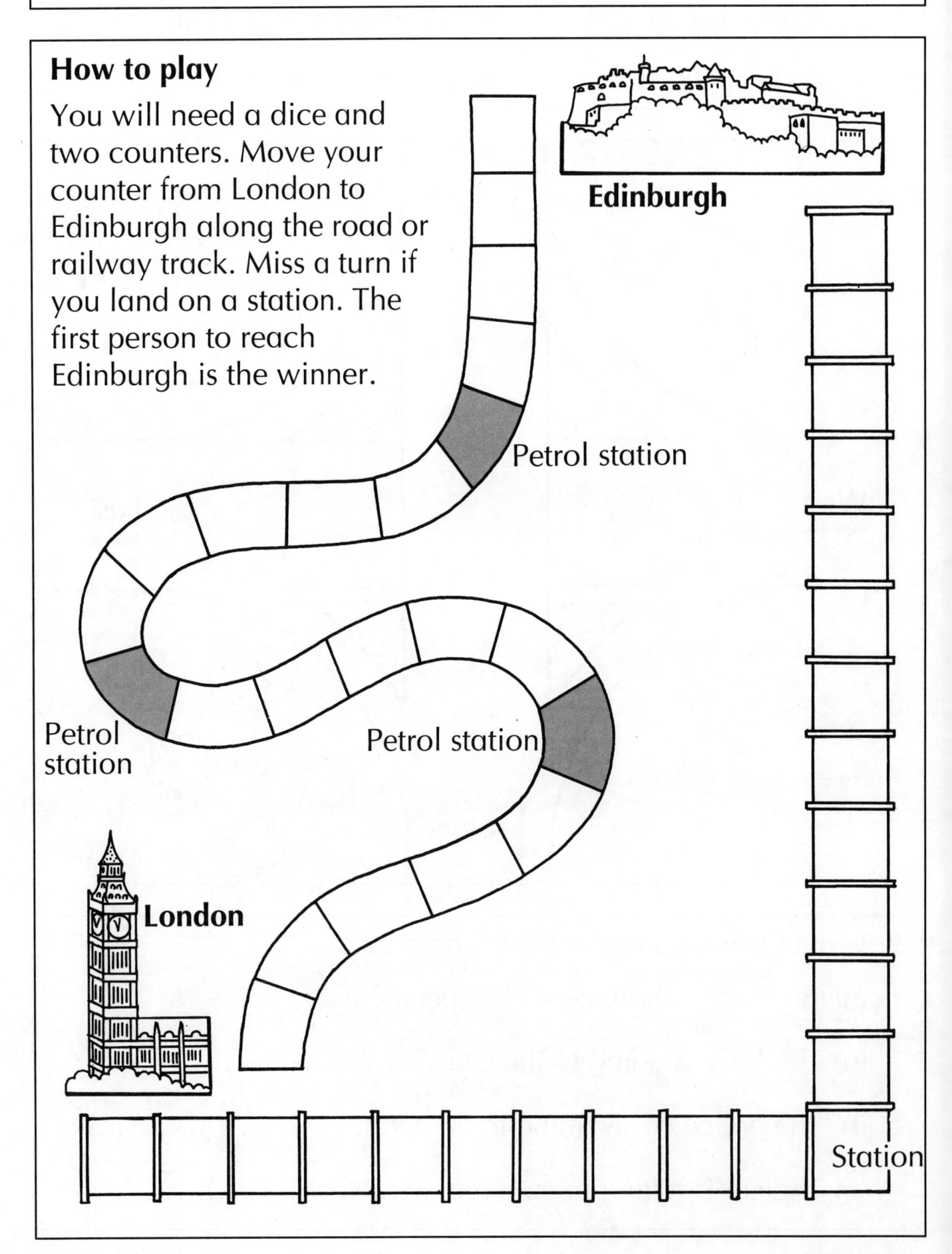

How to play

You will need a dice and two counters. Move your counter from London to Edinburgh along the road or railway track. Miss a turn if you land on a station. The first person to reach Edinburgh is the winner.

Edinburgh

Petrol station

Petrol station

Petrol station

London

Station

Moving around

© 1993 Collins Educational

15 Ships and docks

Name_____

1 Draw a line from the ferry, lorry, car and coach to the right place in the picture.

ferry

car

lorry

coach

2 Colour the pictures.

3 How many ferries can you see? ....

Moving around
© 1993 Collins Educational

16 Planes and airports

Name_____

1. Colour the pointer and world map.
2. Cut out the pointer and world map.
3. Fix the pointer to the map with a split pin.
4. Now make up some journeys.

split pin

pointer

- San Francisco
- Mexico City
- Peking
- Calcutta
- Rio de Janeiro
- Cape Town

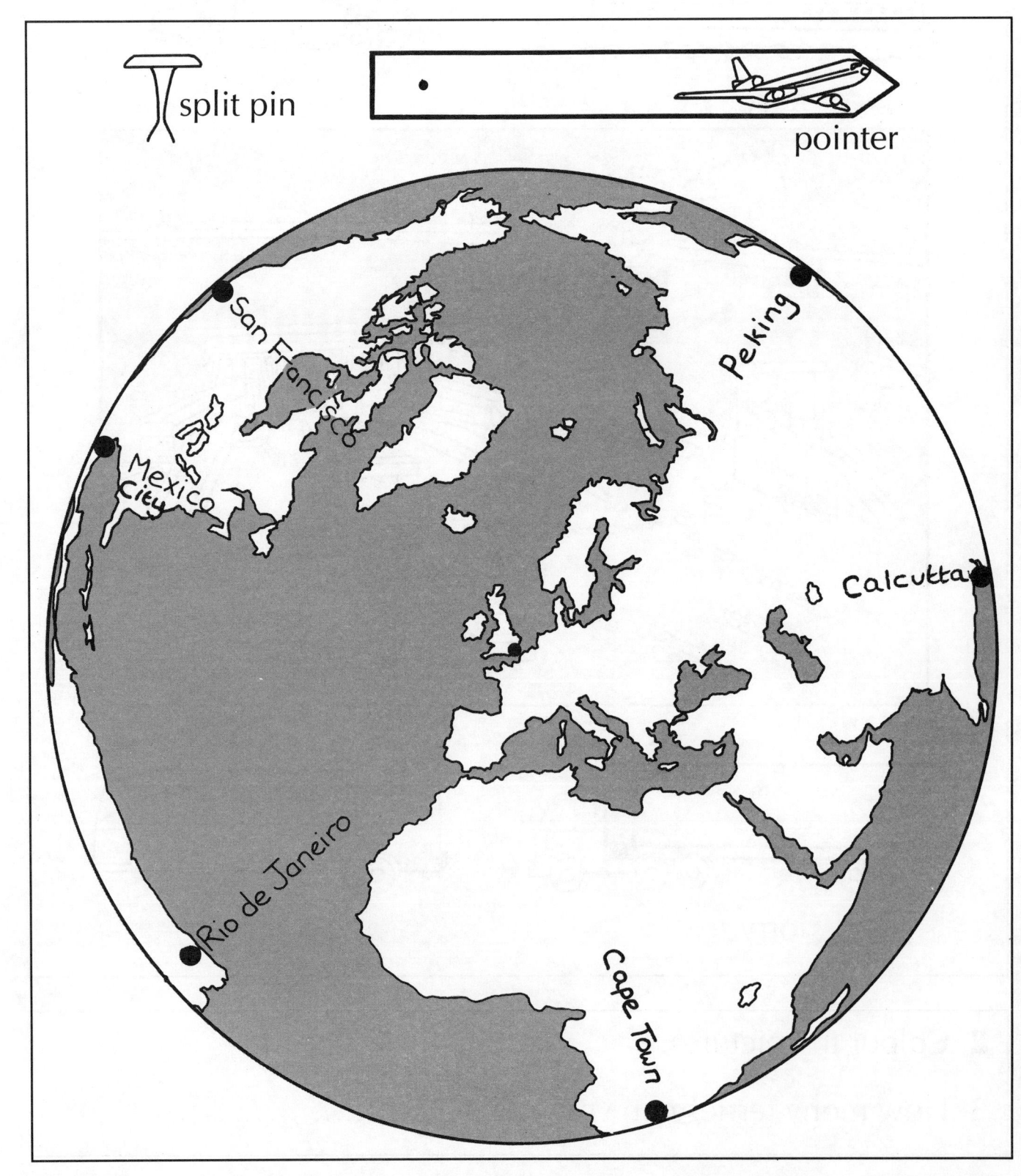

Moving around © 1993 Collins Educational

17 Wet and showery

Name_____

1. Look carefully at the picture. Colour the places blue where you can see water.

2. Colour the rainbow.

The weather

© 1993 Collins Educational

18 Hot and sunny

Name_____

1 Colour the weather symbols.

2 Throw a dice to find out the weather on each day.

3 Draw the right weather symbol.

Dice	Weather	Symbol
⚀	wind	
⚁	sun	
⚂	rain	
⚃	cloud	
⚄	rain	
⚅	sun	

Day	Symbol
Sunday	
Monday	
Tuesday	
Wednesday	
Thursday	
Friday	

4 How many days were sunny? ....

The weather

19 A windy day

Name_____

1 Colour the picture.

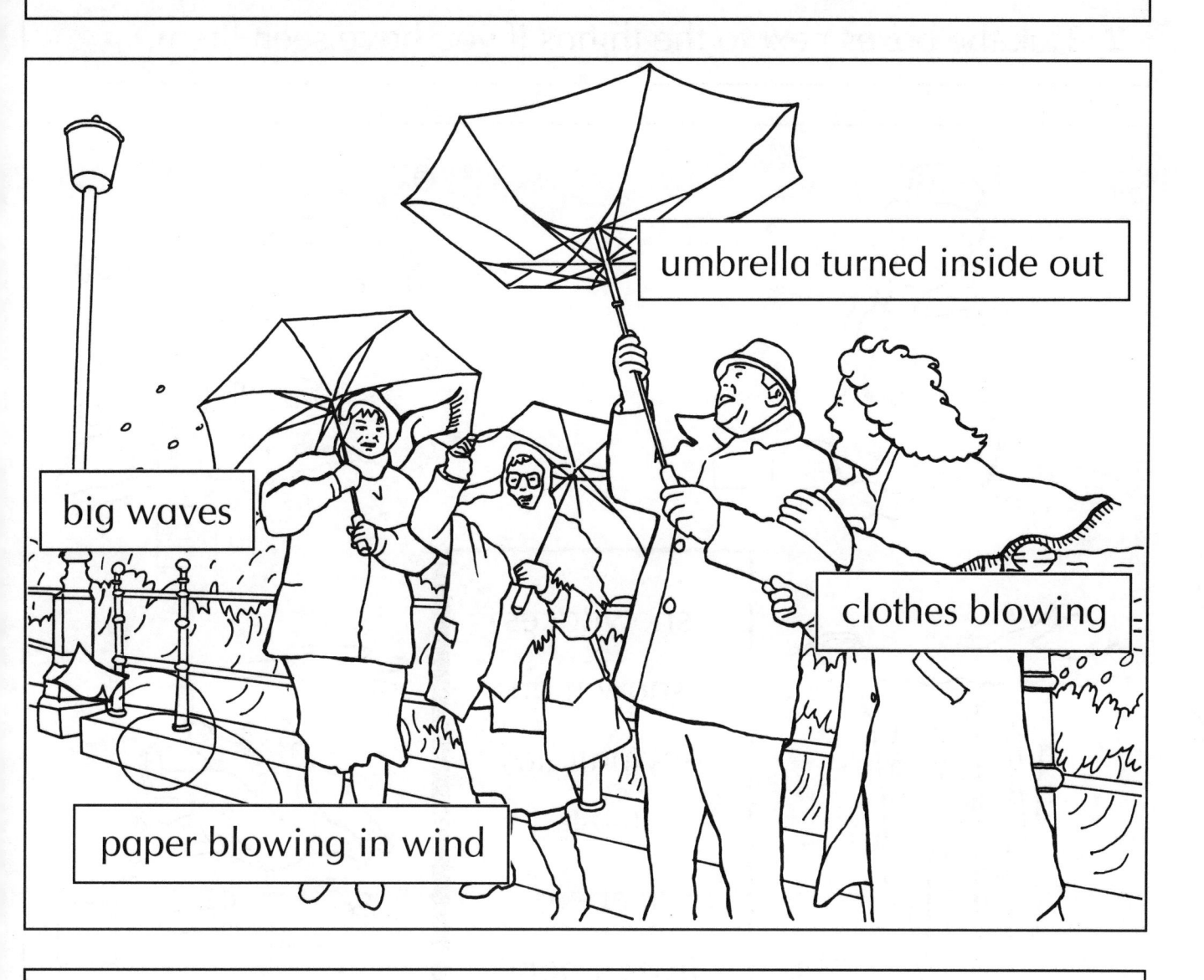

(Picture labels: umbrella turned inside out, big waves, clothes blowing, paper blowing in wind)

2 Make a list of the the things the wind is doing.

a ....

b ....

c ....

d ....

3 How do you feel on a windy day? Circle the best words.

excited   grumpy   happy   nervous   chilly   frightened

The weather © 1993 Collins Educational

20 Freezing cold

Name_____

1. Draw lines linking the words and pictures.
2. Tick the boxes next to the things if you have seen them.

snowflakes

snow man

icy patches

icicle

iceberg

frozen pond

The weather

© 1993 Collins Educational

21 School garden

Name_____

1 Here are three pictures of the same place. Look at them carefully and answer the questions.

What is it like?

....
....
....
....

What has been done?

....
....
....
....

What can you see in the garden?

....
....
....
....

2 What do you have to do to look after the garden?

....

Caring for the environment

22 Recycling

Name_____

1 Colour the routes through the maze.

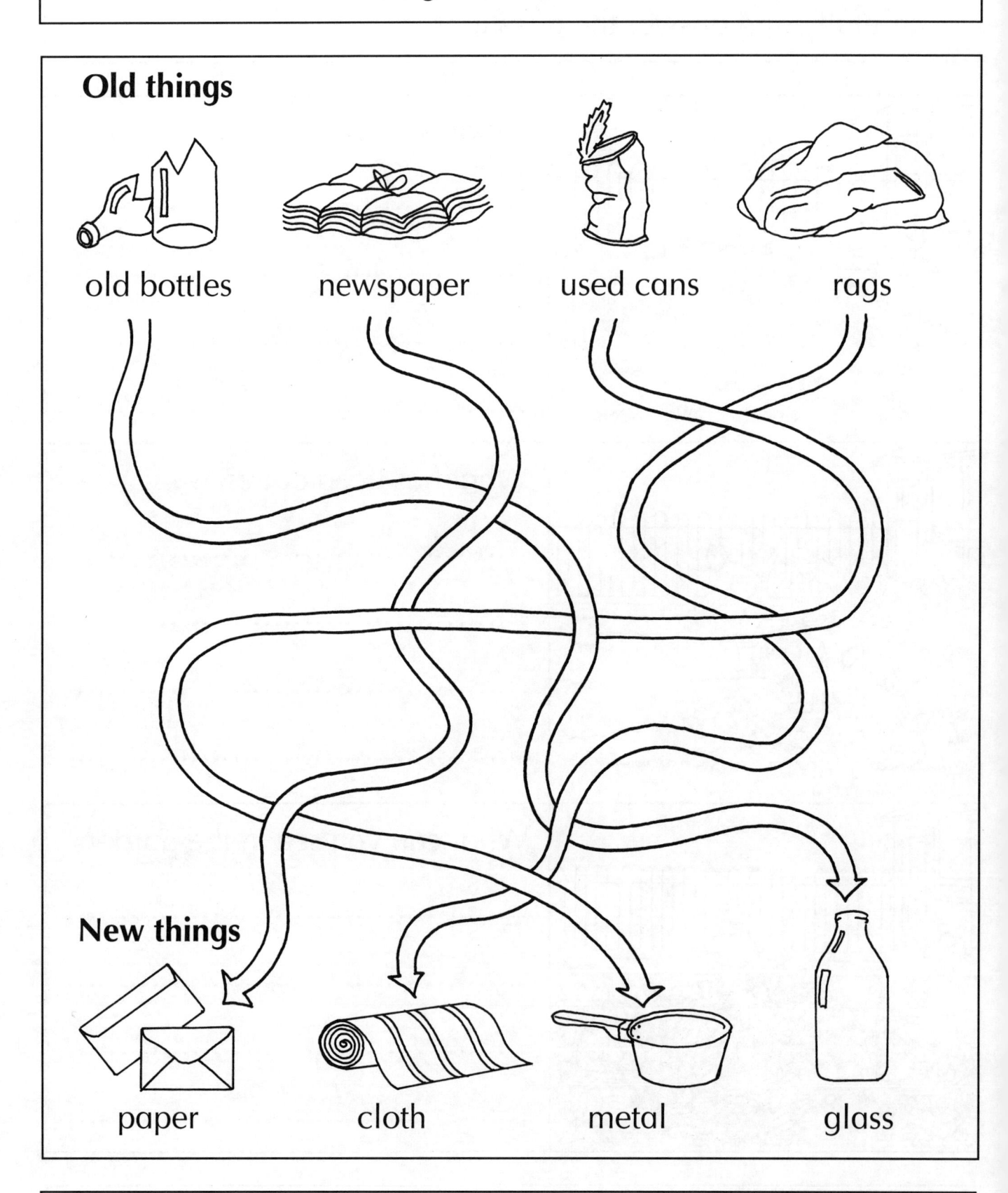

Old things

old bottles   newspaper   used cans   rags

New things

paper   cloth   metal   glass

2 What things do you save for recycling in your home or school? ....

Caring for the environment

© 1993 Collins Educational

23 Looking after buildings   Name_____

1 Tick the boxes to show the places you have visited.

2 Ask four other children if they have been to these places. Tick the boxes in the same way.

windmill

steam railway

castle

cathedral

3 Add up the totals.

4 Which place seems most popular? ....

Caring for the environment   © 1993 Collins Educational

24 Caring for nature

Name_____

1 Colour the picture.

2 Make your own drawing of trees, plants and birds.

| trees | plants | birds |

3 What other creatures might live here?

a .... b ....

Caring for the environment © 1993 Collins Educational

25 The earth from space

Name_____

1 Colour the boxes in the key.

2 Colour the map of the world using these colours.

Key

green	land
blue	sea

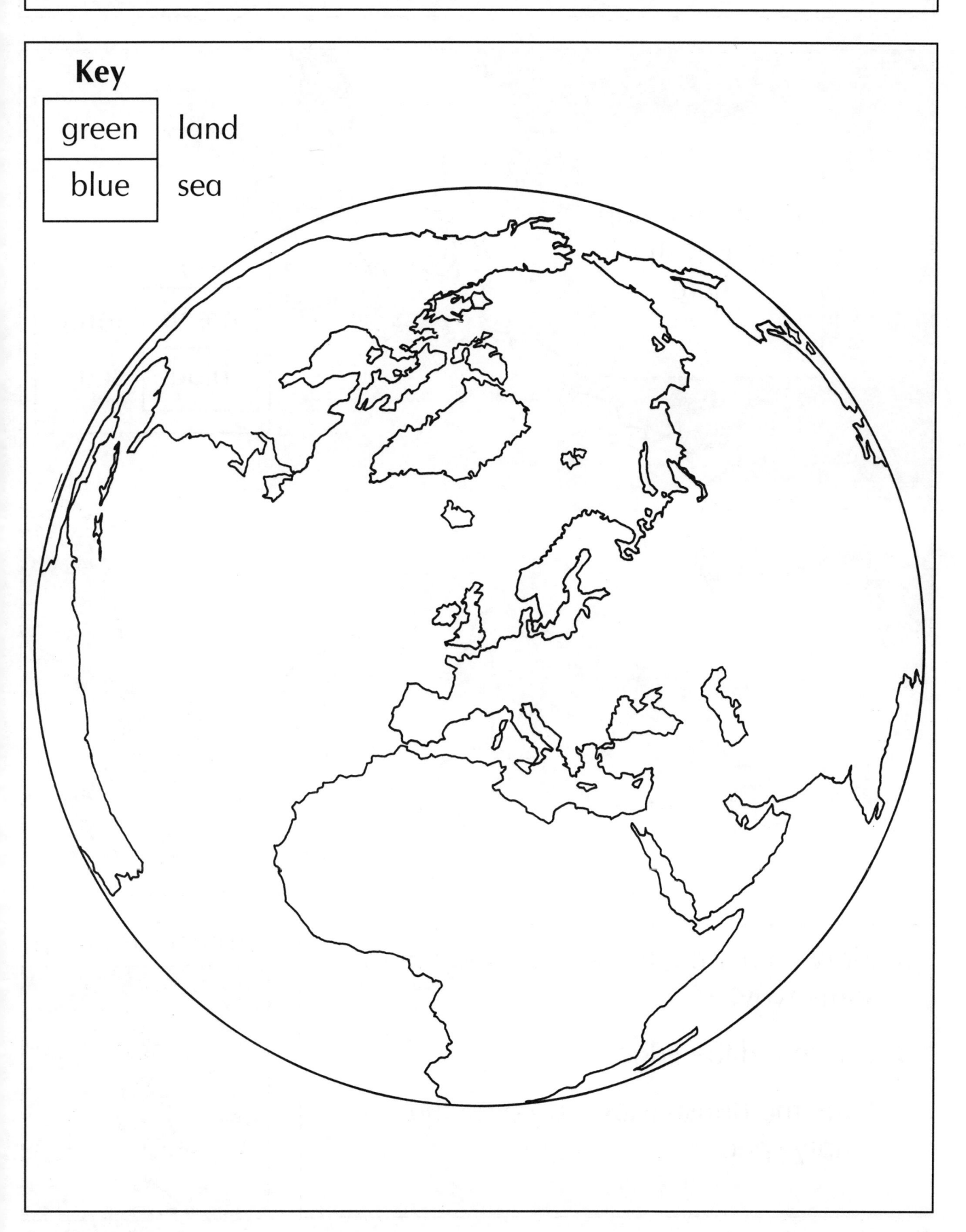

Our planet earth

© 1993 Collins Educational

26 British Isles

Name_____

1. Colour the boxes in the key.
2. Colour the map of Europe using these colours.

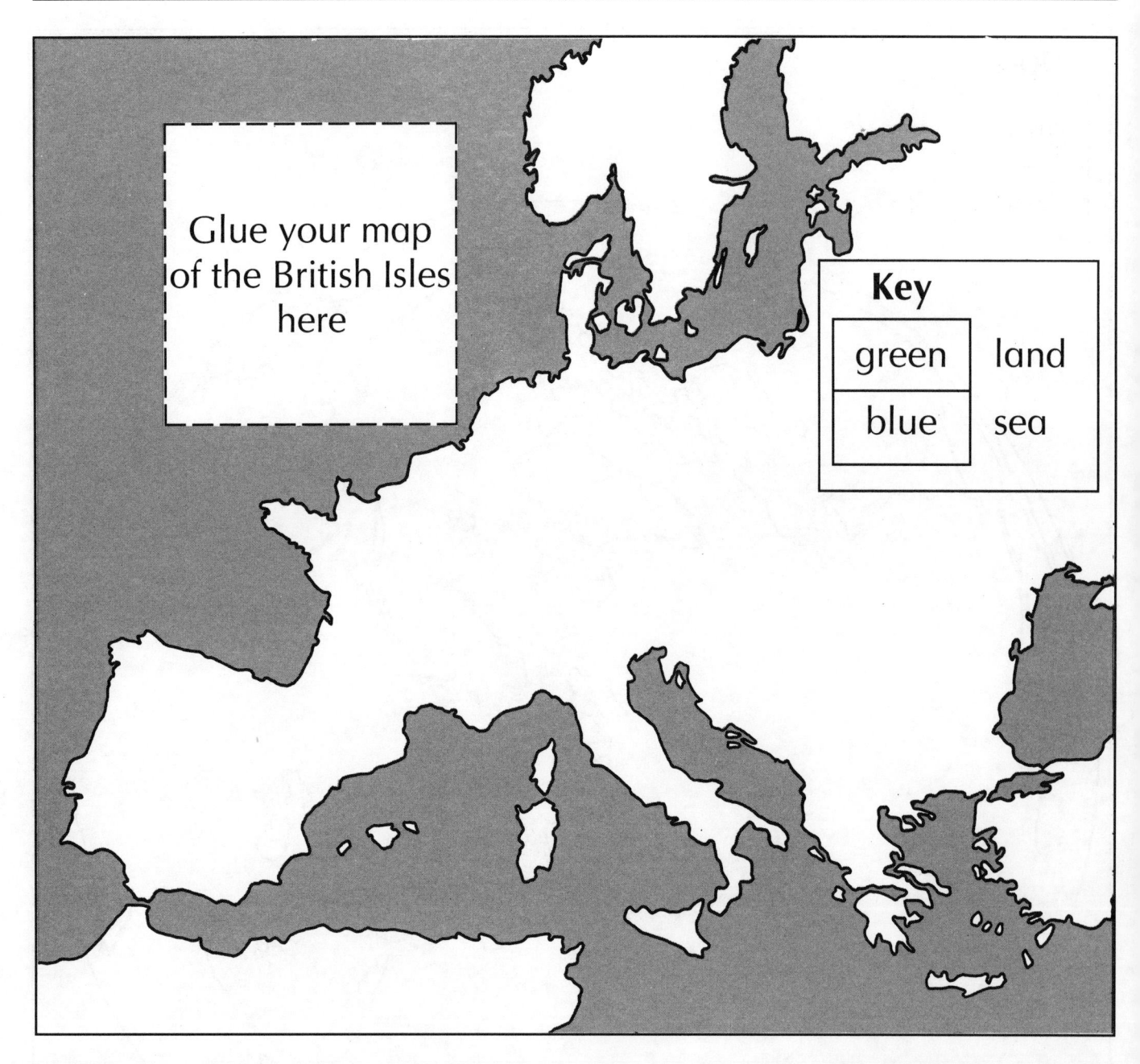

Glue your map of the British Isles here

Key

green	land
blue	sea

3. Now colour the British Isles map in the same way.
4. Cut round the edge.
5. Glue the British Isles map onto the empty space.

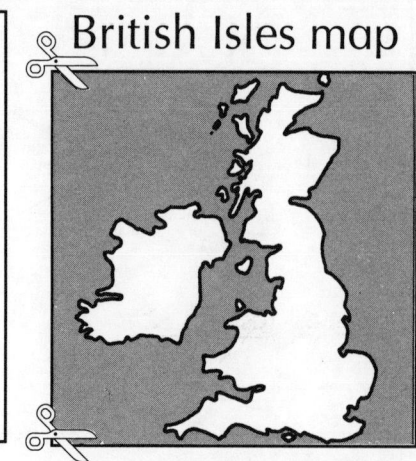

British Isles map

Our planet earth © 1993 Collins Educational

27 Looking down on London   Name_____

> **1** Colour the pictures.   **2** Play the game with a friend.
>
> **How to play:**
> You will each need a dice and six counters.
> Throw the dice in turn.
> Put your counter on the number you have thrown.
> The first person to put down all their counters is the winner.

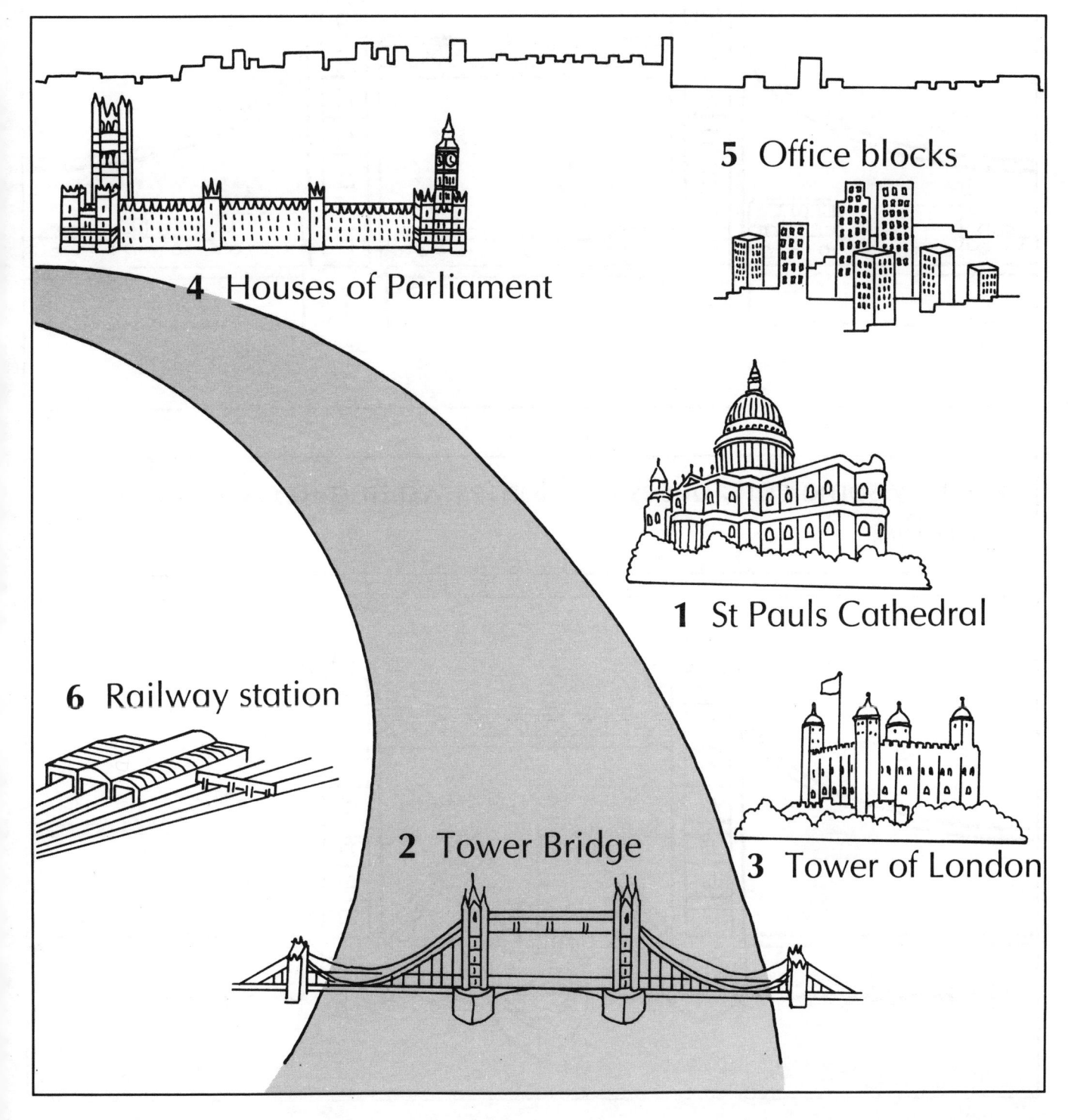

4 Houses of Parliament

5 Office blocks

1 St Pauls Cathedral

6 Railway station

2 Tower Bridge

3 Tower of London

Our planet earth   © 1993 Collins Educational

28 Tower bridge

Name_____

1. Count the cars, buses and lorries on the bridge.
2. Write your answers on the chart.

Chart	
Cars	
Buses	
Lorries	

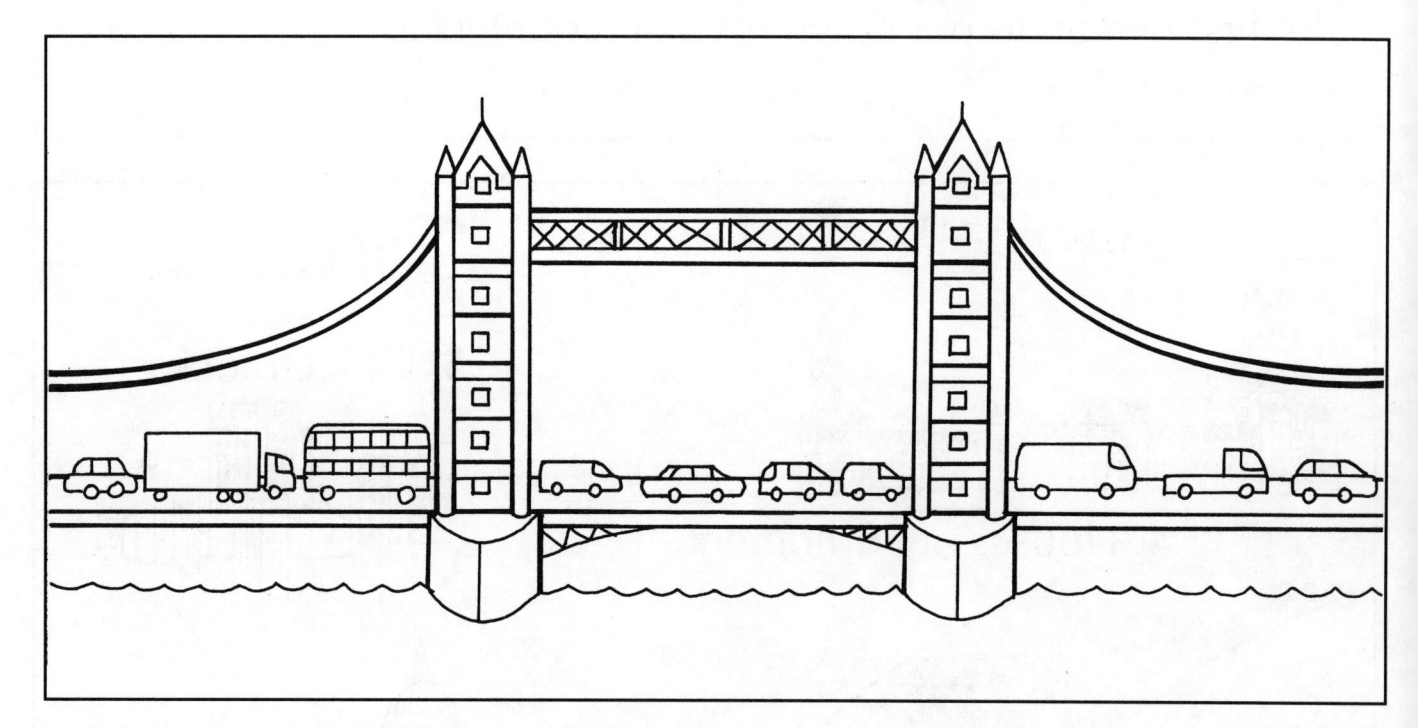

3. Draw some cars, buses and lorries waiting to cross the bridge.

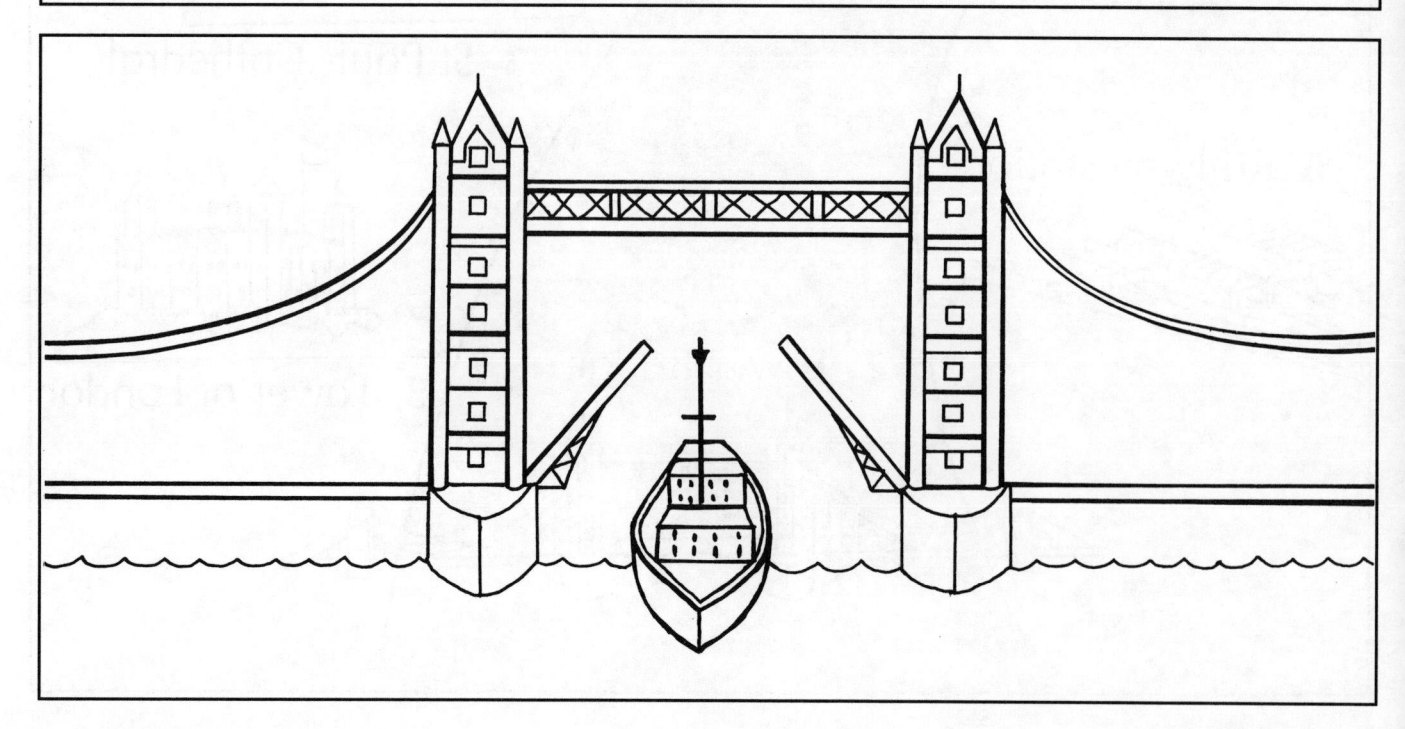

Our planet earth © 1993 Collins Educational

29 The high street

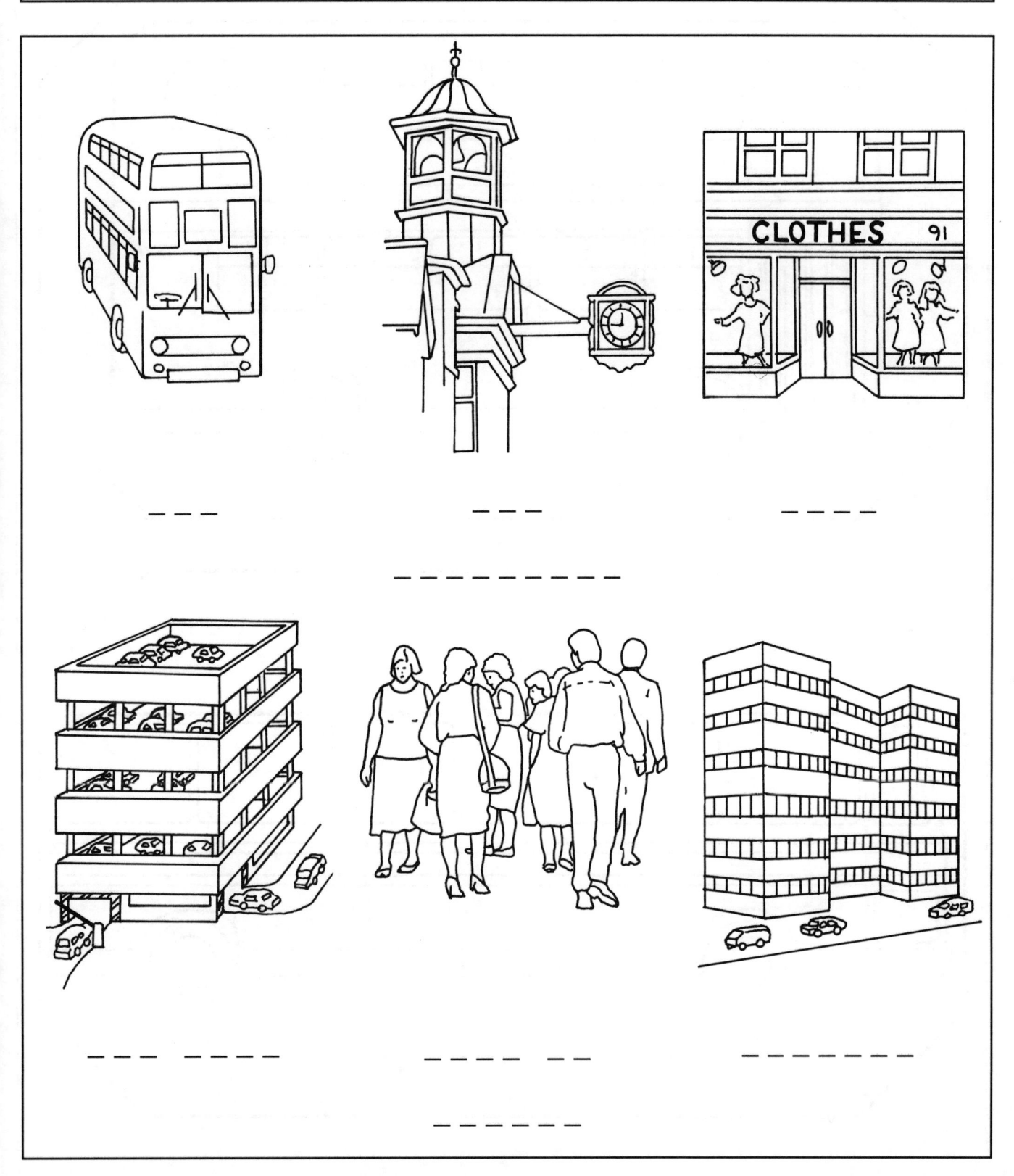

Name_____

1 Colour the pictures.
2 Write the words where they belong.

| bus | lots of people | old buildings |
| shop | car park | offices |

_ _ _   _ _ _   _ _ _ _ _

_ _ _ _ _ _ _ _ _

_ _ _   _ _ _ _ _ _   _ _ _ _ _ _ _

_ _ _ _ _ _

Towns   © 1993 Collins Educational

30 The bus station

Name_____

1. Colour the pictures.
2. Cut them out.
3. Glue them back to back.
4. Make a mobile with other children in your class.

Towns

© 1993 Collins Educational

31 Trading estate

Name_____

1. Colour the model.
2. Cut round the edge and make the slits.
3. Fold along the dotted lines.
4. Glue down the corner tabs.

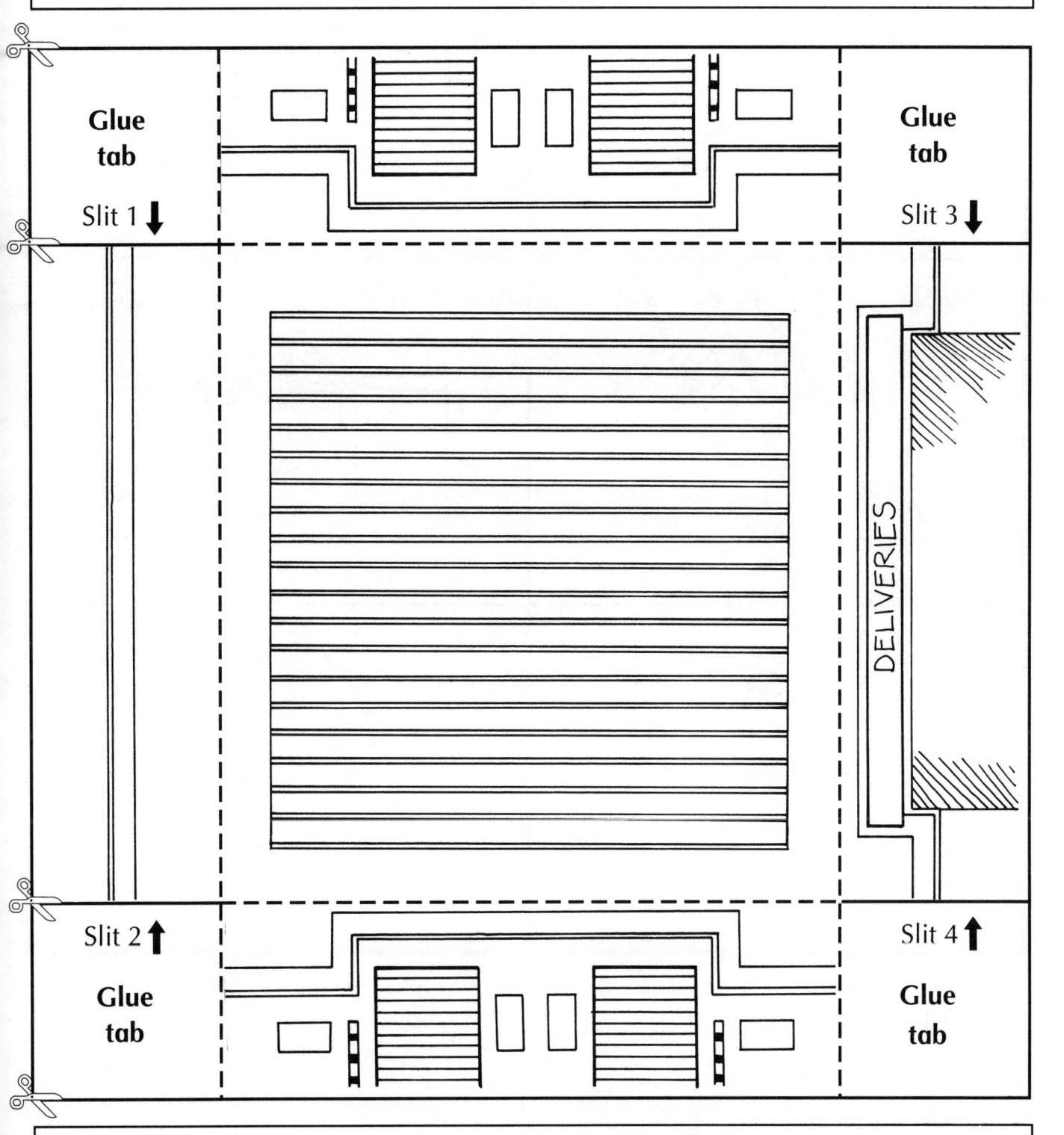

Glue tab

Slit 1 ↓

Glue tab

Slit 3 ↓

DELIVERIES

Slit 2 ↑

Glue tab

Slit 4 ↑

Glue tab

5. Use your model as part of a trading estate.

Towns

© 1993 Collins Educational

32 A sports centre

Name _____

1 Write down the best place for each sport.

  a sports centre   **b** playground

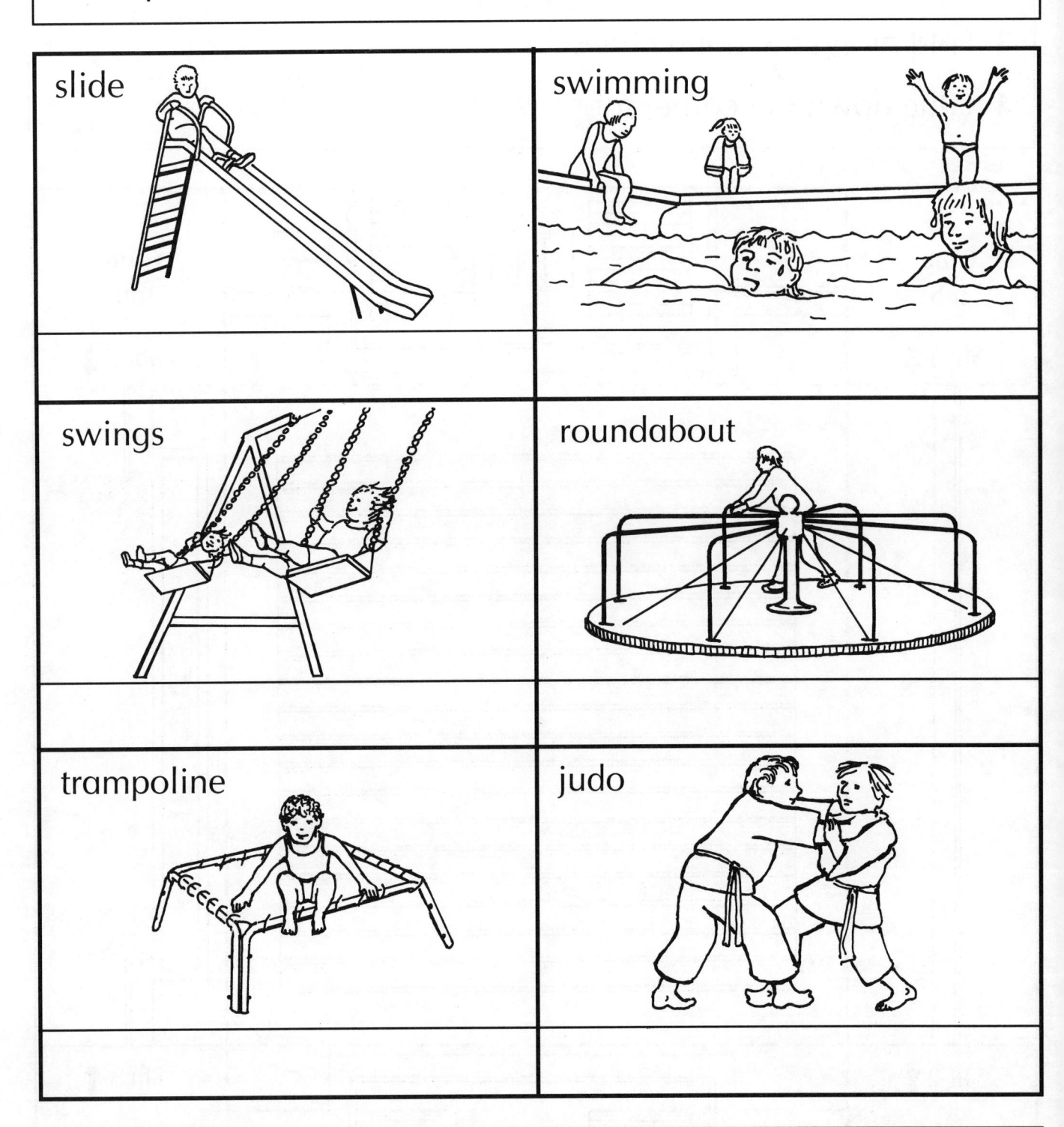

slide	swimming
swings	roundabout
trampoline	judo

2 What else can you do at a sports centre?

....

....

Towns

33 Hills and valleys

Name_____

1 Colour the picture.

2 Write the words where they belong.

    path   valley   hill   field   farm

h _ _ _

f _ _ _ _ _

v _ _ _ _ _ _

f _ _ _

p _ _ _

The countryside

© 1993 Collins Educational

34 In a quarry

Name_____

1 Colour the pictures.

2 Complete each sentence using the right word

coal   food   rock   wood

R _ _ _ comes from a quarry.

W _ _ _ comes from a forest.

C _ _ _ comes from a mine.

F _ _ _ comes from a farm.

The countryside   © 1993 Collins Educational

35 Working on a farm

Name_____

1 Colour the pictures and cut them out.
2 Glue them in the right pairs onto a clean sheet of paper.

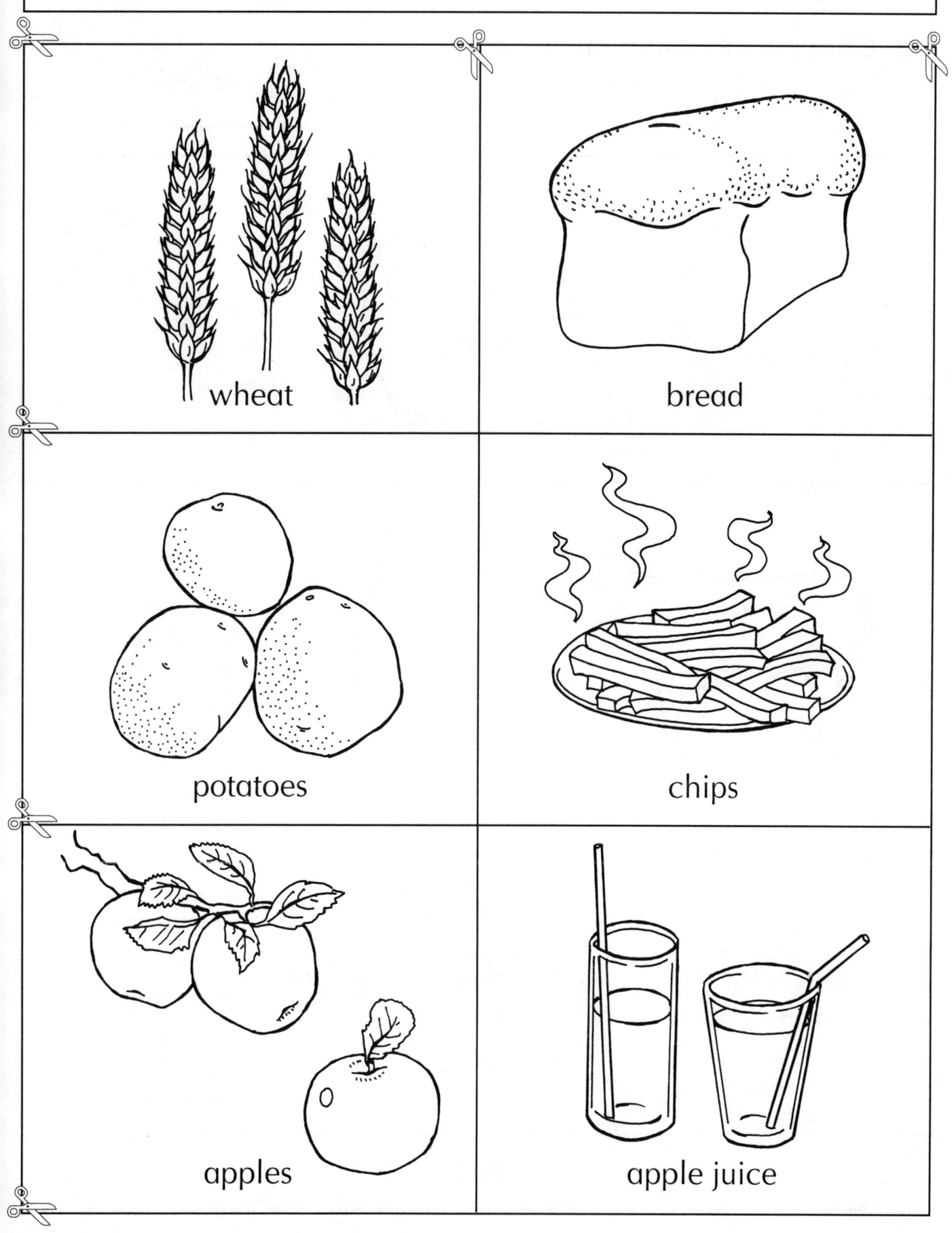

wheat	bread
potatoes	chips
apples	apple juice

The countryside © 1993 Collins Educational

36 A farmer moving sheep   Name_____

1. Colour the pictures.
2. Cut out the sheet and fold along the dotted line.
3. Glue the tab under the top edge.

TAB

The countryside © 1993 Collins Educational

37 Fumes in the air

Name _____

1 Colour the pictures in the circles.

factory chimneys

house chimneys

car exhausts

sprays

2 List four things which pollute the air.

a .... c ....

b .... d ....

Pollution © 1993 Collins Educational

38 A loud noise

Name_____

1 Tick the things which cause a loud noise.
2 Colour the pictures you have ticked.

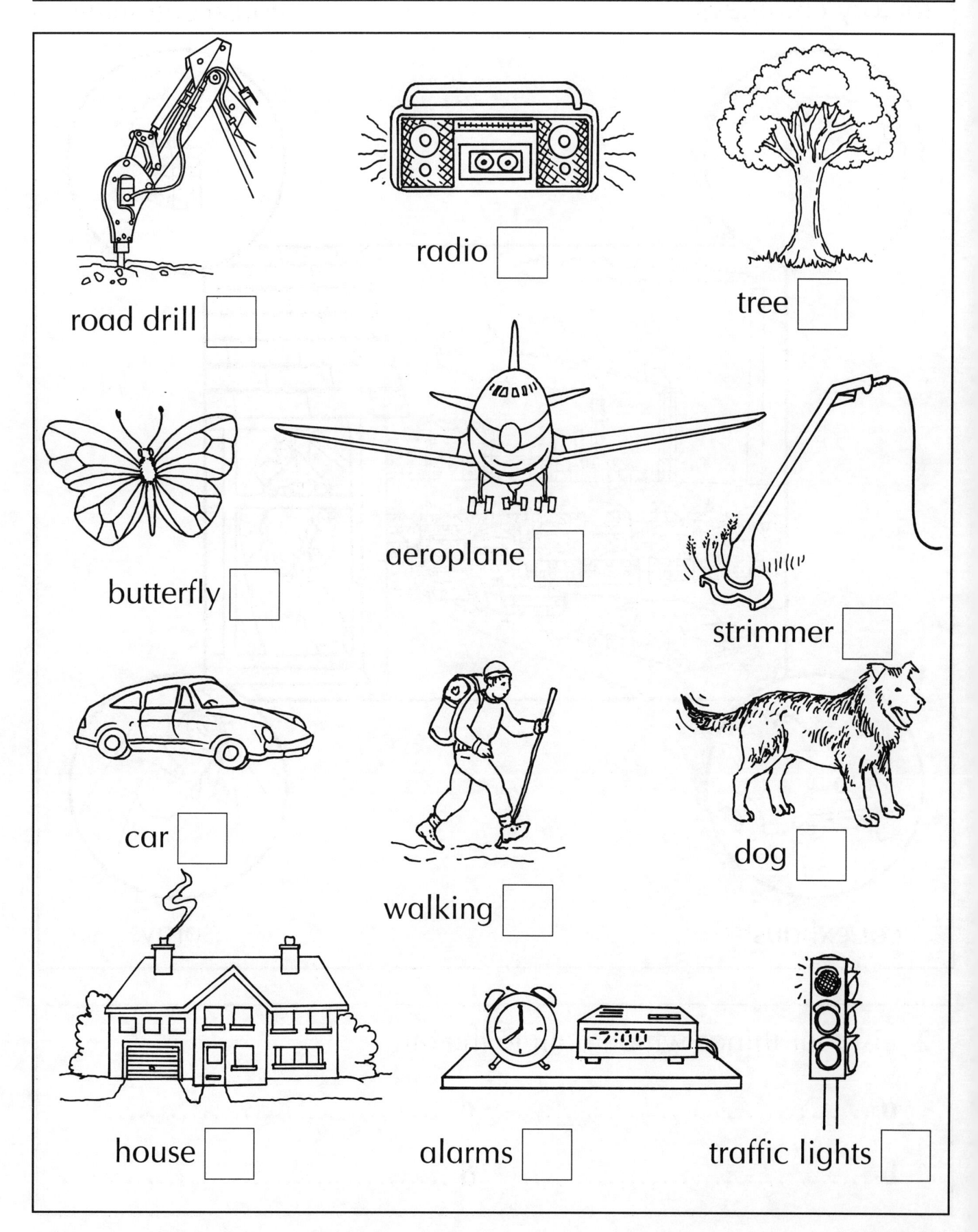

road drill ☐

radio ☐

tree ☐

butterfly ☐

aeroplane ☐

strimmer ☐

car ☐

walking ☐

dog ☐

house ☐

alarms ☐

traffic lights ☐

Pollution

© 1993 Collins Educational

39 A rubbish dump

Name_____

1. Draw a picture of the countryside.
2. Colour it and cut it out.

Picture of the countryside

3. Now draw a picture of lots of rubbish.
4. Colour it and cut it out.

Picture of rubbish

5. Place the picture of rubbish over the bottom of the countryside picture.
6. Tape the bottom edges together to make a flap.

Pollution © 1993 Collins Educational

40 Oil on the beach

Name_____

1 Colour the pictures.

Oil can be useful

It makes buses go.

It keeps houses warm.

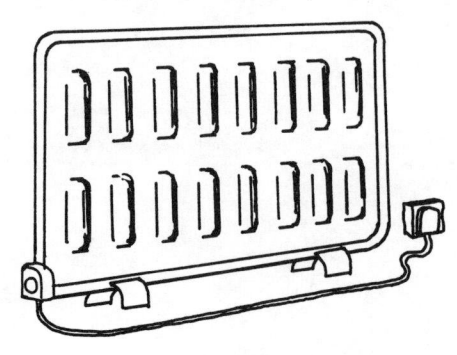

It helps things run smoothly.

Oil causes damage when it spills into the sea

It spoils beaches.

It kills birds.

It kills fishes.

2 Why does oil sometimes spill into the sea?

....

....

Pollution

41 Sandy desert

Name_____

1. Colour the picture of the desert.
2. Draw lines from the words to the things in the picture.

| camel | oil tanks | lorry |

| Arab man | van | sand |

3. Write two words about the weather in the desert.

   a ....   b ....

Other lands

© 1993 Collins Educational

42 Rainforest

Name_____

1. Colour the pictures of the creatures that live in a rainforest.
2. Cut them out.
3. Use them in a large rainforest picture of your own.

parrot

butterfly

crocodile

leopard

monkey

turtle

Other lands

© 1993 Collins Educational

43 Polar lands

Name _____

1 Draw what the penguins can see.

2 Write two words about the weather in polar lands.

a .... b ....

44 High mountains

Name_____

1. Colour the mountain and foothills.
2. Cut out the mountain, foothills and snow cap.
3. Dress the mountain. Place the snow cap and foothills over the mountain and fold back the tabs.

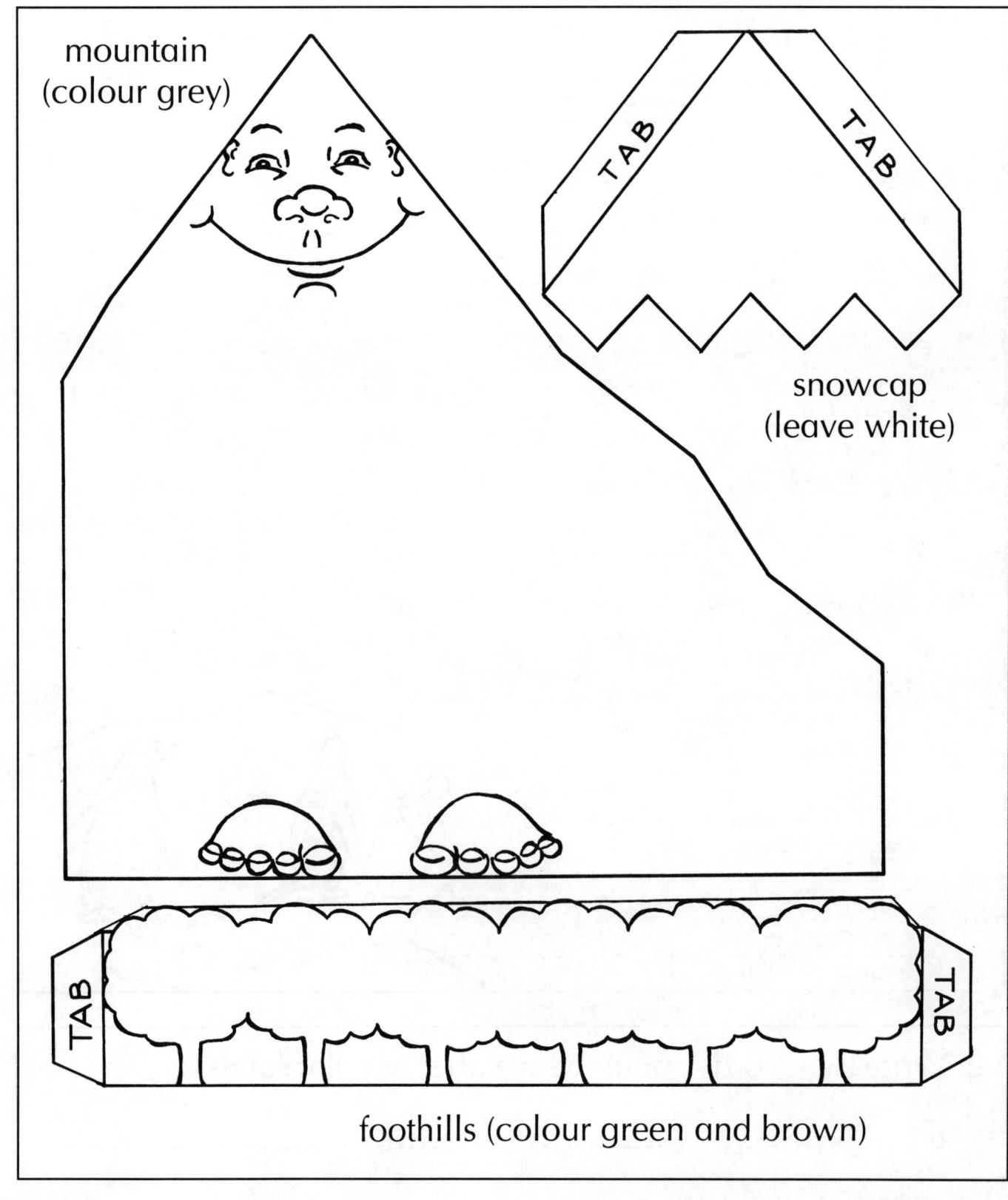

mountain
(colour grey)

TAB TAB

snowcap
(leave white)

TAB TAB

foothills (colour green and brown)

Other lands

© 1993 Collins Educational

45 Getting food ready

Name _____

1 Write each sentence under the right picture.

These are lovely cakes.   The rice is ready to pick.

Bring some wood for the fire.   We are getting food ready.

1

2

3

4

Children around the world © 1993 Collins Educational

46 Watering the fields

Name _____

1 Draw lines from the words to the right pictures.

sailing   swimming   toilet   watering fields

drinking   playing   cooking   washing

2 How is water being used in photograph 46?

a ....   b ....

Children around the world   © 1993 Collins Educational

47 A family festival

Name_____

1 Write the names of the festivals where they belong.

Christmas   Diwali   Chinese New Year   Eid

Birth of Christ

C _ _ _ _ _ _ _ _

Festival of Light

D _ _ _ _ _

Spring Festival

C _ _ _ _ _ _ _ N _ _
Y _ _ _

Thanks to God

E _ _

2 How are festivals special?

....

....

Children around the world   © 1993 Collins Educational

48 An outdoor school

Name _____

1 Colour the picture.

2 Answer each question by ticking the right box.

Are the children sitting in the shade?

Yes ☐   No ☐

Does the weather look hot?

Yes ☐   No ☐

Are the children wearing uniform?

Yes ☐   No ☐

Can you read the words on the blackboard?

Yes ☐   No ☐

3 Where in the world do you think this might be?

....

Children around the world

49 Plans

Name_____

1. Cut out the drawings of the teacher and children.
2. Find the place where you think they sit.
3. Glue their pictures on to the plan.

| Mrs Evans | Jonathan | Krishna and Wendy | Paul, Susan and Jack |

computer

Mrs Evans' desk

playhouse

children's desk

Map skills

© 1993 Collins Educational

50 Directions

Name_____

1 Colour the pictures.   2 Cut them out.

3 Take the picture of your table and put it in the middle of a large sheet of paper.

4 Put the pictures round the edge to match your classroom.

5 Glue them down.

6 Draw arrows from your table to the other drawings.

your table

door

teacher's desk

sink

bookcase

window

Map skills

51 Symbols

Name_____

1 Colour the symbols.

2 Write the words where they belong.

| mountain | church | bridge |
| rain | snow | sunshine |

Places	Weather

Map skills

© 1993 Collins Educational

52 Routes

Name_____

1. Find the route from home to school.
2. Colour the route.
3. Write 1 at the first place you pass. Write 2 at the second place. Then 3. Then 4.
4. Fill in the numbers and names at the bottom of the page.

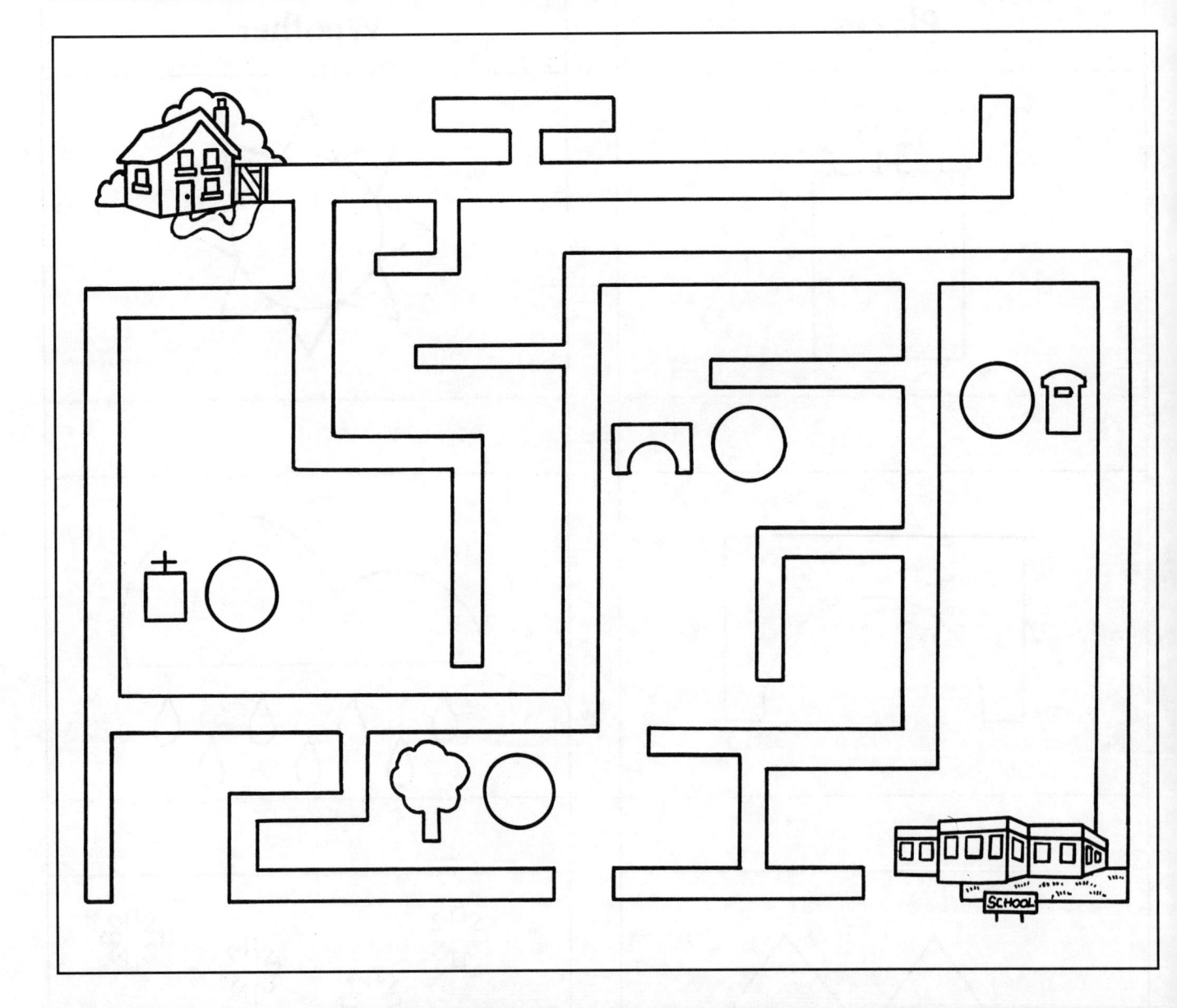

Symbol	Number	Landmark
☩		
🌳		

Symbol	Number	Landmark
🌉		
🚪		

Map skills

© 1993 Collins Educational

53 Grids

Name_____

1 Colour the squares to make a picture

Green	Brown	Blue
A1 B1 B4 B5 B6 C1 C4 C5 C6 D1 D4 D5 D6 E1 E4 E5 E6 F1	C2 C3 D2 D3	A2 A3 A4 A5 A6 B2 B3 E2 E3 F2 F3 F4 F5 F6

Map skills © 1993 Collins Educational

54 Compass points

Name_____

1 Colour the compass model.   2 Cut out the compass.

3 Fix the 'needle' to the model with a paper fastener.

4 Use your model to find out about compass points in and around your school.

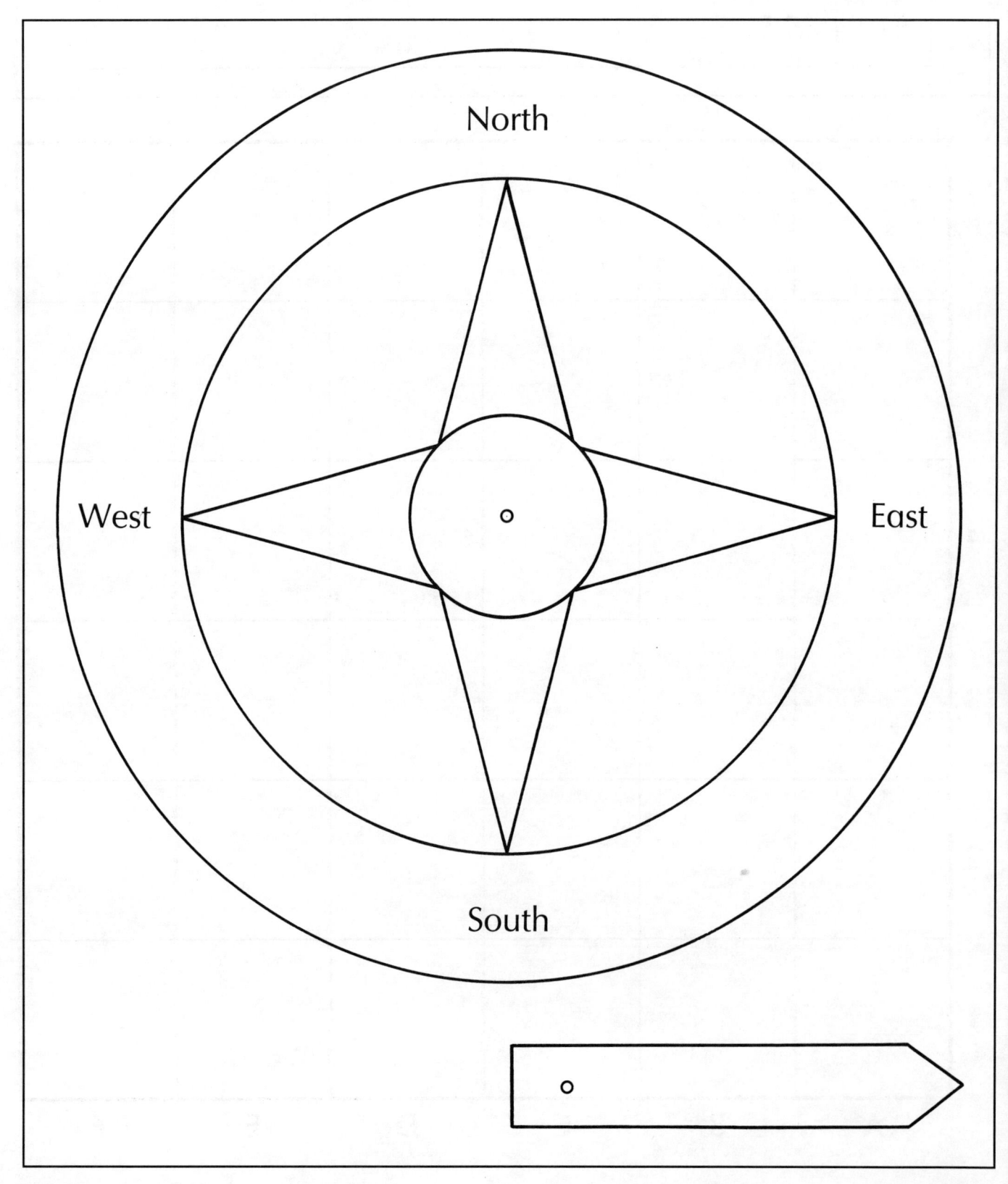

North

West

East

South

Map skills

© 1993 Collins Educational

55 The United Kingdom

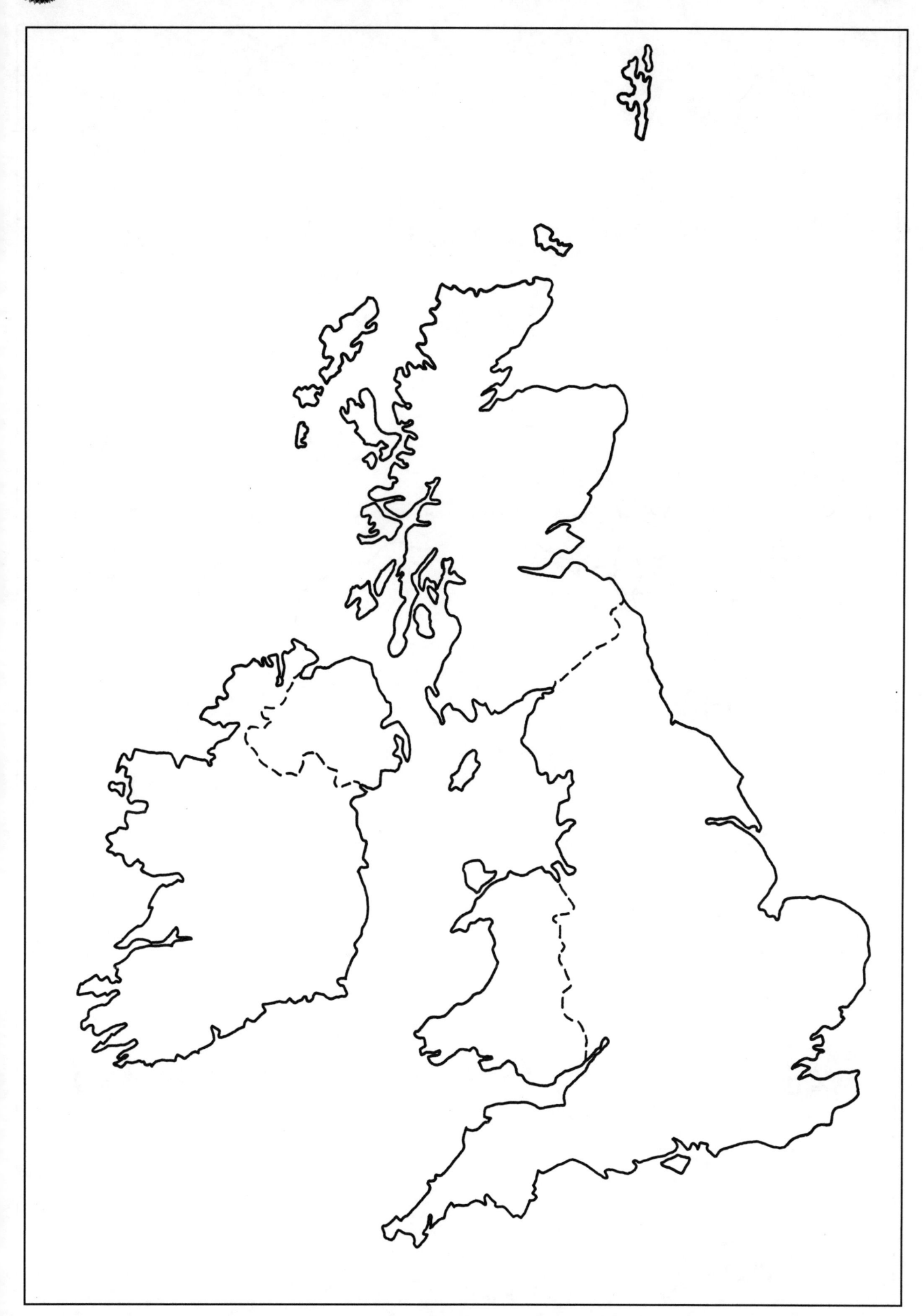

Name_____

Map skills

© 1993 Collins Educational

56 The world

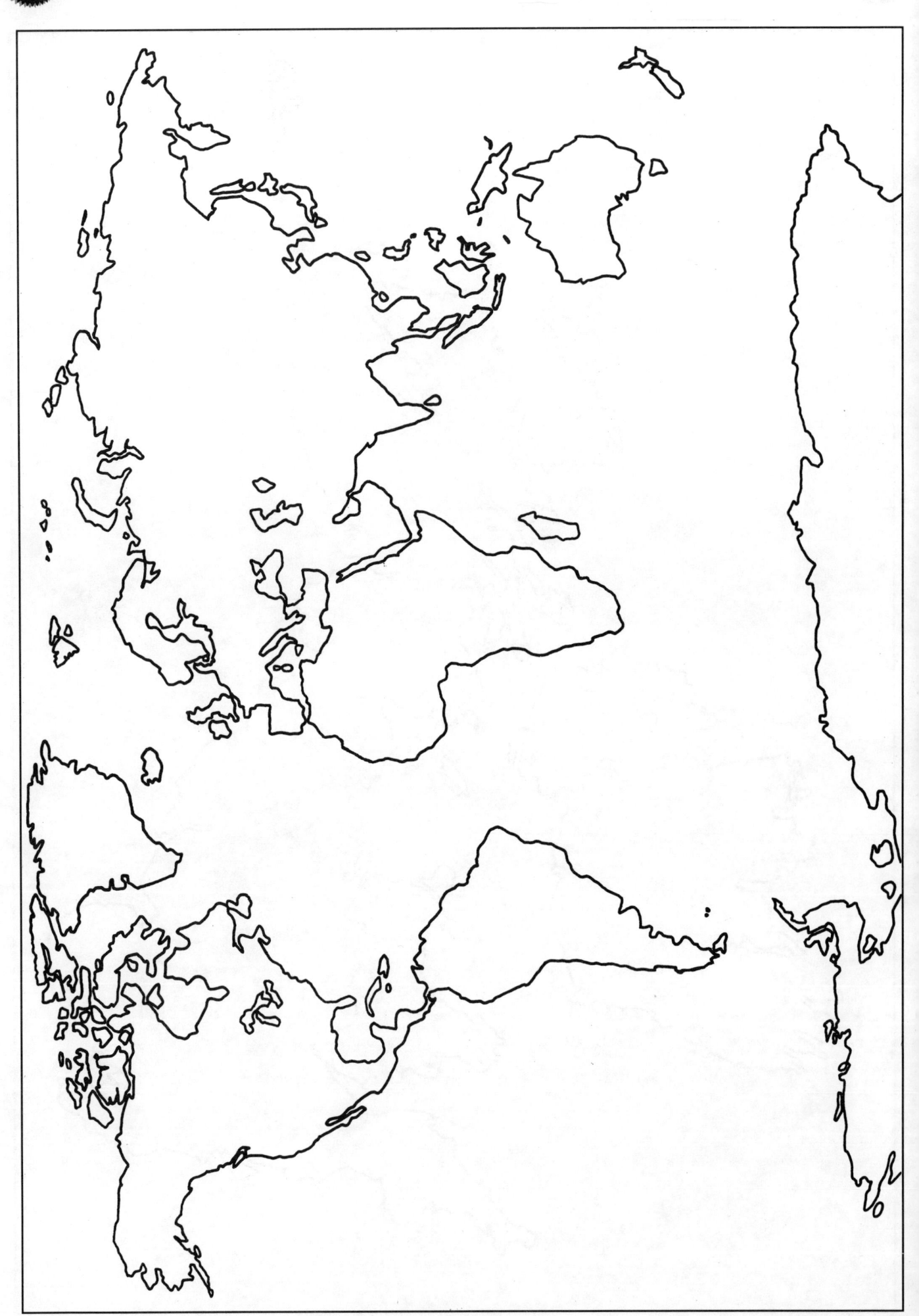

Name_____

Map skills

© 1993 Collins Educational